DORSET
CHURCH WALKS

Diana Pé

Published by *PP (Pé Publishing)*
Email: Tonype@onetel.com

ISBN 978-095436905-7

Cover illustration: Audrey Stevens
Other illustrations: Doreen Peskett
Maps: Brian Panton, BDP Associates

Photographs: Diana Pé

Printed by: Downland Print Services Ltd, 2010

Disclaimer: the information in this book is given in good faith and is believed to be correct at the time of publication. No responsibility is accepted by the author and publisher for errors or omissions, or for any loss or injury howsoever caused. Only you can judge your own fitness, competence and experience.

About this book

Churches

The churches in this book are cared for by local villagers who have generously left most of them open so that we may share in their peace and beauty. Please cover your boots before entering (plastic bags and elastic bands are useful for this purpose).

Also, have you heard of The Churches Conservation Trust, a charity which has saved 300 churches for the nation? Five churches in this book have been sensitively restored and maintained by the Trust. They are at Winterborne Tomson in Walk 2, Nether Cerne in Walk 15, Whitcombe and Winterborne Came both in Walk 34 and Tarrant Crawford in Walk 37. For more information telephone 020 936 2285 or write to The Churches Conservation Trust, 89, Fleet St, London, EC4Y 1DH.

Maps

The sketch maps are only a guide, they are not to scale. You need a copy of the Ordnance Survey map, recommended at the top of each walk. Explorer maps are up to date and quite detailed.

Acknowledgements

I should like to record my gratitude to the following for their help in the preparation of this book: John Avenell, Gabrielle Ma, Tony and Jean Gillman, Robert Pé, Tony Pe, Sally Peltier, Viviane Pfitzner, Kate Prince, Kathleen Ramsay, Audrey Stevens, Peggy Synge, Caroline Wilberforce and Cynthia and Miles Wilson.

Members of the Dorset branch of the Ramblers Association, who checked the walks and offered valuable advice and suggestions for improvements, are: Mr G. Hemsley, Mrs R. Bramah, Mrs S. Blake, Mrs L. Carry, Mr G. Bull, Mr M. Heckford, Mr A. Combridge and Mr B. Panton.

Dorset County Council Rights of Way team has been helpful in answering queries and in carrying out work on some of the footpaths used in this book. There is sterling work in progress to improve the footpaths of Dorset.

Mid Dorset

Self-catering cottage and B & B: Manor House Farm, Ibberton, Near Blandford Forum, DT11 OEN. Tel: 01258 817349. Owners: Mr and Mrs Old.

Self-catering annexe: Gold Hill Organic Farm, Child Okeford, Blandford Forum, DT11 8HB. Tel: 01258 860293. Owners: Mr and Mrs Cross.

West Dorset

A wildlife centre offering courses and accommodation: The Kingcombe Centre, Toller Porcorum, Dorchester, DT2 OEQ. Tel: 01300 320684 Fax: 01300 321409. Director: Mr Nigel Spring.

Fernhill Hotel, Charmouth, Bridport, DT6 6BX. Tel: 01297 560492 Fax: 01297 561173.

North Dorset

B & B, also meals kitchen: Talbot Hotel, Iwerne Minster, Blandford Forum, DT11 8QN. Tel: 01747 811269. Manager: Mr Mark Richardson.

South Dorset

Swanage Youth Hostel, Cluny Crescent, Swanage, BH19 2BS. Tel: 01929 422113

Contents

Introduction

The Walks

Five Walks near Blandford Forum

Five Walks near Bridport

Five Walks near Dorchester:

Five Walks near Shaftesbury:

Five Walks near Sherborne:

Five Walks near Wareham

Five Walks near Weymouth

Five Walks near Wimborne Minster

SOMERSET

Yeovil

• 22. Trent

Sherborne

River Yeo

• 21. Folke

DORSET

25. •

Hazel-
-bury
Bryan

River Axe

Stoke
Abbott

• Beaminster

DEVON

• 15. Cerne
Abbas

• 9. Netherbury

River Brit

• Wootton Fitzpaine

River
Piddle

8. Symondsbury

• 7. Charmouth •

11. Charminste

Bridport

Lyme
Regis

• 6. Shipton
Gorge

Dorchester

• 10.
Winterbourne
Steapleton

34. •
W. Knighton

• 31.
Bincombe
Down

Abbotsbury •

35. Langton
• Herring

Wey-
-mouth

Portland

WILTSHIRE

Gillingham

17. West Stour

16. Shaftesbury

19. Compton Abbas

18. Fontmell Magna

23. Hinton St Mary

Sturminster Newton

24. Iwerne Courtney

1. Shillingstone

38. Tarrant Hinton

HAMPSHIRE

Cranborne

20. Edmondsham

40. Knowlton

5. Okeford Hill

4. Ibberton Hill

Blandford Forum

39. Tarrant Rushton

River Avon

Ringwood

14. Hilton

3. Milton Abbas

River Stour

28. Winterborne Whitechurch

Sturminster Marshall

37.

36. Wimborne Minster

12. Milborne St. Andrew

2. Almer

Bere Regis

13. Tincleton

River Frome

Poole

Bournemouth

Christchurch

Wool

26. Wareham

32. Holworth

33. East Lulworth

Studland

27. Corfe Castle

29. Steeple

Swanage

Lulworth Cove

30 Worth Matravers

St Aldhelm's Head

Introduction

Most people pass through Dorset on their way to Devon and Cornwall. Those of us who love the county are happy to be left here in a varied and powerful landscape. Dorset has a primeval, haunting quality. Neolithic hill forts and burial places abound. Early fortificactions along the coast and on the inland hills keep Dorset separate. Bokerly Dyke in the north-east is 4 miles long and was built by the Romans to protect the farmland there. The pagan past of Dorset lurks below the many tumuli on the Dorset hills. Neolithic works lie below the Iron Age defences of Maiden Castle, the largest prehistoric hill fort. It stands south-west of Dorchester. Hambledon Hill, north of Blandford Forum has a Stone Age long barrow near the Iron Age fort. Pilsdon Pen, the highest point in Dorset has a small Iron Age earthwork. Hammiton Hill east of Bridport has the oldest Bronze Age barrows. Weatherby Castle near Milborne St Andrew and Chalbury near Weymouth are Iron Age forts. Woodbury Hill near Bere Regis is an Iron Age fort and in medieval times was the setting for outdoor fairs. King Henry III granted a charter in 1231 and Woodbury Hill Fair became the largest in the south of England. It could last a week; there was Wholesale Day, then Gentle Folks Day, All Folks Day, Sheep Fair Day and, lastly, Sale Day. 'Greenhill' in Thomas Hardy's 'Far From The Madding Crowd' represents Woodbury Hill.

A Pagan Past

The Wessex Ridgeway passes on the high ground of Dorset. It is thought to be part of an ancient highway that linked Devon to the east coast, possibly 4000 years ago. In the hills of Cranborne Chase, the pagan past surfaces at the Dorset Cursus, the longest Neolithic track in England. It was a processional route with rectangular enclosures at either end. The Iwerne Valley running north south from Fontmell to Hod Hill, has rich remains of Stone Age, Celtic, Roman and Saxon times. The pagan past of Dorset triumphs at nearby Knowlton where three prehistoric enclosures encircle the ruined church. The pagan past is in the wind that blows over the cliffs in the south. It inhabits the forests and moorland and is captured in the doom-laden novels of Thomas Hardy.

The meanings of the many resounding place names of Dorset can be traced back to their Celtic, Roman or Saxon roots. 'Tarrant' is Celtic for 'liable to flood', 'Fontmell' is also Celtic; 'font' is a spring and 'mell' comes from 'moel', a bare hill – so 'spring by the bare hill' seems to be the meaning. 'Stikel' is Saxon for 'steep' and one of the Winterborne villages is called

'Stikland'. 'Belchalwell' is another Saxon name, explained in walk 5. 'Bega' was a Saxon saint who gave her name to Beaminster.

Knights favoured by William the Conqueror have left their names to many villages. Hammoon was the domain of the De Mohuns; Sixpenny Handley of Saxpena and Sutton Waldron of Waleran. Hazelbury Bryan means the hazel wood held by De Bryan. Guy de Bryan, who bought the manor in 1361, was a descendant of De Brione.

The towns of Dorset are small and friendly. Eight of them are the bases of the walks of this book. **Shaftesbury**, to the north-east, is the only hill town. It has extensive views south over the rich meadows of Blackmore Vale and north to the Quantocks and Mendips. This was probably the site of the Celtic town of Caer Palladore. West of Shaftesbury lies the beautiful golden town of **Sherborne** in the Yeo Valley and close to Blackmore Vale. Besides the dominant Abbey, dating back to AD 705, Sherborne has other medieval buildings including a castle. Further south the town of **Blandford Forum** has medieval origins.

The great fire of 1731 destroyed many old buildings and gave the town the opportunity to rebuild in Georgian red brick and stone. Blandford's central position in East Dorset makes it ideal in its role as a small market town. Another little market town, managing not to be swamped by Poole and Bournemouth is **Wimborne Minster**. The twin-towered Minster escaped the ravages of the Dissolution and dominates the town. Romans probably had a base here but the first records are post Roman. In AD 705 a Benedictine nunnery was built on this site. Come south-west of Wimborne and you will find the old port of **Wareham** which also has a Roman past. In the Church of the Lady St Mary are 6th- and 7th-century stones, evidence of Anglo-Roman Christianity. The small county town of **Dorchester** goes back to Roman times when it was called Durnovaria. From medieval days it has been a market town. The Romans took over Maiden Castle, the hill fort to the south, in AD 43 and they made our next town, **Weymouth**, their port. Fishing vessels and pleasure craft use the port of today. On the Melcombe side of the port there are Georgian houses which remind us that Weymouth was a favourite bathing place of George III when bathing machines were all the rage. **Bridport** is the most westerly of our centres. Near here the Romans grew hemp, used to make rope. This brought prosperity and in Norman times Bridport had its own mint, priory and 120 houses. These houses have gone; the oldest building now is the 14th-century Chantry House. There are several Georgian buildings, including the town hall. The River Brit goes through Bridport on its way to the sea, one and a half miles away.

The Romans named the people of Dorset the 'Durotriges'. They brought with them both Roman gods and also the new religion, Christianity. A mosaic, discovered at Hinton St Mary is believed to represent the oldest known head of Christ. He shares the picture with classical mythology; Bellerophon spearing Chimaera. The mosaic is in the British Museum. Other relics of Roman-Christianity have been found in Wareham and Frampton. Christianity also absorbed the local pagan religiion. Some churches stand in places sacred to Stoneage Man. In AD 601 Pope Gregory the Great wrote to Bishop Mellitus instructing him to retain temples and convert them to the service of God. In this way the religious aura of the site was exploited. Knowlton church, in the middle of prehistoric circles is a prime example. In Shillingstone church, an interesting coffin lid has been discovered. 'Shillingston Slab' depicts a Saxon lord. There are a sun and a moon on either side of the head. These are pagan symbols but here it is believed to be an appeal to Christ as 'the Light of the World' and to the Virgin Mary as the 'moon godess'.

Christian churches

Some of the first 'churches' were stone crosses erected at crossroads or near a river crossing. There is one beside the Weymouth Road near Langton Herring. New Anglo-Saxon and Norman churches were often built next to the many manor houses of Dorset. The Lord of the Manor, his family and serfs worshipped in these chapels which give the impression that they are private. Bingham's Melcombe is one such example; the Manor is screened from our view but fortunately the church has a footpath and is included in this book.

The Saxons embraced the Christian religion. The pattern of church parishes today is a legacy from that period. The wooden Saxon churches have not survived in Dorset. Several churches contain Saxon stonework: the doorways of Loders and Sherborne Abbey, the long and short work in St Martin's, Wareham and ancient relics in Whitcombe and Lady St Mary, Wareham. This, the largest Saxon church in the country, survived intact until 1842 when the Victorians remodelled it! The Saxons also founded monasteries and nunneries: Abbotsbury, Cerne, Milton and Shaftesbury.

The Normans rebuilt many of the churches and enforced a stricter discipline in the monasteries. They also created new religious bodies; the largest Cistercian nunnery in England was founded in 13th century at Tarrant Crawford. Where is it now? Where is Shaftesbury? The monasteries in Dorset, as elsewhere in England, suffered under Henry VIII. Dorset has several Norman churches: St Aldhelm's Chapel and Worth Matravers near Corfe, Studland on the cliffs near Swanage, St Catherine's on the slopes opposite Milton Abbey and the modest little gem, Winterborne Thomson with a curved apse. The churches at Bere Regis, Charminster and Iwerne Minster have Norman arcades. Gussage St Andrew has a Norman nave and Tarrant Crawford a Norman chancel. The ruined Knowlton church also dates from the 12th century. Several interesting Norman fonts exist, including Nether Cerne, Puddletown and Wareham St Mary. There are Norman doorways at Milborne St Andrew and Whitchurch Canonicorum.

Many churches have lancet windows of the Early English period and Whitchurch Canonicorum has a fine arcade in that style. But perhaps the most typical feature of Dorset churches is the solid, Perpendicular tower. Beaminster is generally thought to have the finest tower in Dorset but there are many close rivals.

A few handsome Georgian churches, designed by John and William Bastard include Blandford Forum, Charlton Marshall and possibly Wimborne St Giles. On Portland, a local mason, Thomas Gilbert designed the Church of St George which has been compared with St Paul's, London.

Between Dorchester and Wareham, a memorable and beautiful Georgian Gothic church is at Moreton. The 'new' Fleet church west of Weymouth is Victorian Gothic. See 'West Sussex Church Walks' (Sigma Press) for a summary of the different styles of church architectecture and illustrative sketches.

Geology and stonework

Dorset is a county of great geological diversity and has provided an extraordinary amount of different kinds of stone for building. There is sandy moorland in the south-east, clays and sand in the south-west, chalk downland in the middle. The north is the most fertile with extensive pasture lane over Blackmore Vale. The many little rivers of Dorset wind through fields, past hills and woodland and over plains to the sea. The Stour is the chief river. Into it run the Tarrant, the Winterborne, the Allen and Moors rivers. It enters the sea at Christchurch Harbour. The Frome carries its tributaries, Sydling Water and the Cerne to Poole Harbour at Wareham, where it is joined by the River Puddle or Trent. The little rivers Wey, Brit, Char and Lim enter the sea at Weymouth, West Bay, Bridport, Charmouth and Lyme Regis respectively.

The most famous stone of Dorset is **Portland**, which is a very durable grey limestone, a type of Oolite. It has been used locally since at least the 14th century. It became famous in 17th century and was greatly in demand by Inigo Jones and Christopher Wren. The Isle of Portland, near Weymouth is one huge rock pitted with quarries.

Purbeck stone, formed when crocodiles and dinosaurs roamed here, has a distinctive pattern of fossilised snail shells. The Romans quarried Purbeck 'marble' and discovered that it does not last well outside but it can be polished to resemble real marble. It has been widely used indoors, especially between 1170 and 1350 AD. Many churches contain effigies and sculptures in Purbeck marble. On the other hand, Purbeck quarries have yielded the most durable and heaviest of stone slates. House roofs have tended to sag under their weight and much mortar has been needed to flush them up.

There is also a stone, known as **Purbeck-Portland**, considered the toughest of all. It used to be quarried at Winspit from mine shafts inclining toward the sea. This quarry is now closed; the expense was too great. To visit this disused quarry as well as a working quarry see Walk 30.

Lias is a limestone which follows the belt of Oolite stones. Blue Lias was quarried on the Devon-Dorset border and has been much used in Lyme Regis. The interesting, quirky shape of hills hereabouts is caused by the underlying Lias.

Inferior Oolite, a grainy limestone occurs in north-west and south-west Dorset. It has been used throughout Sherborne where its pale cream colour contrasts with the golden Ham Hill stone brought from Somerset. Also in the north, quarries near Todber and Marnhull have provided a biscuit coloured stone as the houses bear witness. In the south, Abbotsbury has a limestone similar to that of Todber but with more fossils in the stone. Nearby Portesham stone has a white limestone.

There is a rusty brown stone, **Abbotsbury Ironstone**. Heathstones in East Dorset also have a rich brown colour derived from iron. They were valued for the contrast they give with other stones and have been used in the churches of the Winterborne and Tarrant valleys. The Minster at Wimborne is a remarkable example of contrasting stones.

Greensand, with the green iron-bearing mineral, glaucomite, is from north and west Dorset. Shaftesbury Upper Greensand has been locally used since Saxon times. It can still be seen in Gold Hill in the old retaining wall to the Abbey. It has been transported on the River Stour as far as Wimborne. Sturminster Newton church is built entirely of Shaftesbury Greensand. In the west it is usually the Chert from the upper Greensand which has been used. Chert is similar to flint, very hard but often silvery blue or light tan in colour. Iron Age men used Chert cobs to build forts such as Pilsdon Pen, Lamberts Castle and Coneys Castle. Some buildings in Lyme Regis, including the Cobb, are of Chert. An interesting and unusual use of split Chert can be seen in Catherston Leweston church near Charmouth. Carstone, a coarse brown stone comes from the lower veins of Greensand, found more in Hampshire.

In the south-west, **Forest Marble**, a strong, shelly grey limestone was quarried at Bothenhampton near Bridport. It has been used for building many houses and rope factories in Bridport and can be seen in Beaminster, Charmouth and Whitchurch Canonicorum. There were also quarries at Langton Herring and West Fleet. The old church at Fleet is built entirely of

Forest Marble. Forest Marble has been used for dressed stone; thick pieces cut for ashlar and thin ones for roofing.

Ashlar is cut from a thick smooth stone. It is used for building with little mortar. Portland and Shaftesbury sandstone are also suitable for ashlar. Rubble is a stone which has been broken then dressed to shape by the mason.

Flints come from the central chalk downlands of Dorset. They are hard and uneven, good for outside weatherproofing but need structural support of stone or brick at corners and edges. Sometimes flints are split to give a flat surface and occasionally they are knapped square.

Builders in Dorset, including builders of churches have made the most of the great variety of stones. Sometimes a combination of stones gives a mottled effect as in the brown and grey of Wimborne Minster. Other builders have chosen alternating bands of flint and sandstone. Some have a pattern: one square of flints one square of rubble stone. Knowlton church has a combination of flint, Greensand and dark heathstone.

Masons in Dorset have been very skilled both in cutting and shaping stones and in designing and decorating buildings. Angels, flowers, leaves, human shapes have all been cleverly carved. They have also had fun in using their imaginations to shape grotesque monsters, human and animal, from stone. Some of these gargoyles carry water spouts, others are decorative or intended to frighten away devils.

Wherever possible, in the description of each church, I have mentioned the types of stones used.

Winterborne Clenston has an elegant,
solitary church that stands south of the manor house. (See Walk 3)

Five Walks near Blandford Forum

Walk 1

Shillingstone – Child Okeford – Hambledon Hill – Hod Hill – Stourpaine – Durweston – Bryanston – Blandford Forum

This is a linear walk. Catch a bus from Blandford Forum to Shillingstone, a 15-minute ride, then walk back to base. From the ancient busy village of Shillingstone, we cross the River Stour and head for downland. Ahead is a magnificent stretch of the walk along Hambledon Hill, an Iron Age hill fort with massive ramparts and wonderful views. It is the home of buzzards which nest in the trees on the east side. Hod Hill is smaller and has its own charm. We come back down to cross the river again and take lane and woodland paths through the grounds of Bryanston School back to Blandford Forum. Child Okeford church is also included in Walk 24, Sherborne Section

Starting point: Shillingstone church; GR 824115

Maps: Explorer 117, 118 and 129; Landranger 194

Distance: 9 miles

Public transport: at the time of writing, Damory Coaches (01258 452545) buses run from Blandford Forum to Shillingstone. Bus 190, Friday 9.10 am; Bus 309, weekdays 8.40 am and 1.40 p.m and Saturday 7.15 and 11.40 am; Bus 310 Monday and Thursday, 10 am Saturday 7.45 am and 12.20 pm

Terrain: varied, from meadows to hills and woodland

The Churches

Holy Rood, Shillingstone, is a welcome haven from A357, which roars the length of the village. The church is to the east and has a view of Hambledon Hill. A 7th-century wooden church was burnt down in the 9th or 10th century, probably by the Danes. The lords of the manor in the 12th century, the Eskellings gave their name to the village. The present flint church is mainly Norman with an ashlar-faced Perpendicular tower. Norman windows are high in the nave and north in the chancel. The fine roof decoration (1902-03) is by G.F. Bodley, architect of Washington Cathedral. The square Norman font is of Purbeck marble. The Shillingstone slab (see Introduction page 3) is an important relic, evidence of Pagan influence on Christianity.

St Nicholas, Child Okeford, is built of alternating bands of flint and stone. The Perpendicular tower is of greensand. Inside, the recently refurbished church is spacious and handsome with marble faced walls. Outside, Hambledon Hill invites you to climb its impressive slopes to admire the natural wonders and the earthworks of ancient tribes.

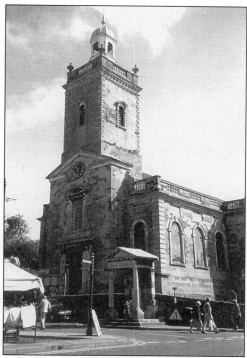

Blandford Forum has an impressive Georgian church at the market place

Stourpaine, Holy Trinity stands at the edge of the village between the River Stour and Hod Hill. This is an Iron Age hill fort with a Roman fort in the north-west corner. South-east of Hod Hill at Great Bournes, a prosperous Roman villa once stood in Constantine's reign. Nearby Lazerton was once a separate parish but could not support a rector and was amalgamated with Stourpaine in 1431. Stourpaine also suffered poverty and the church decayed to such an extent that it had to be rebuilt in 1858. Again, here is a flint church with a greensand ashlar tower. The tower and two north windows are Perpendicular. The window next to them is in Decorated style.

St Nicholas, Durweston, on the other side of the river, is another flint and stone church with an ashlar tower. An interesting feature of the tower is the presence of holy images in niches, one above the other. The present church is Victorian, built in 1847 in Early English and Perpendicular styles.

Saint Peter and Saint Paul, Blandford Forum, is the greatest work of the local brothers, John Bastard 1687-1770 and William Bastard 1689-1766. They created fine Georgian buildings in the neighbourhood. This church was built to replace an earlier one burnt in the fire which raged through Blandford Forum in 1731. The original design for the church shows a spire on the high tower. Now it has a small cupola instead. Most of the stone used is Wiltshire greensand ashlar. It is soft and tended to flake. Fortunately, support has come from the window frames, quoins and pilasters which are of Ham Hill and Portland stone. Huge columns inside the church with Ionic capitals are of Portland stone. The apsidal east end is particularly beautiful. The whole church; nave, chancel, north and south aisle is spacious and magnificent.

The Walk

Shillingstone church can be seen from the main road. It stands behind the village school. From the church, follow the main access path back to the little roundabout. Take the road straight on. This curves quietly through the back of the village. Turn left at the first opportunity and go gently down Hine Town Lane as far as a footpath on the left. This leads across the old railway and down to the River Stour. *After rain this path may be muddy. The worst of this can be avoided by continuing down Hine Town Lane as far as the sports ground. Enter by the gate on your left and cross the field to the railway line. Turn left and walk along the railway line to the gates of the footpath crossing. Turn right.* Ahead Hambledon Hill rises impressively. A fine new footbridge spans the river.

Go across the River Stour then turn left, heading north and make for the farm gate. In the next field, continue on course and cross a farm track, enclosed by hedges. Once through these, you will see a stone barn ahead. You are separated from the barn by a hedge. Hug the hedge on your right for 50 metres then go through the swing gate to another track which leads into Child Okeford. Turn left and follow this track as it bends left to the west of the village. Turn right at the tarmac road and up to the main village street. Child Okeford church, village stores and pubs are up on the left.

Our route to Hambledon Hill is straight on along a wide track opposite. A footpath crosses the end of the track. Turn right and head south-east along a footpath bordered by trees on the right and a fenced meadow on the left. In about 200 metres this path joins the road at a point where it also meets the bridleway to Hambledon Hill. Turn left up the bridleway, following the curve along the southern ramparts of Hambledon Hill. Pass the trig. point at the top and turn right and south along a track on the top of the world. In 200 metres avoid the turning to the right. Hod Hill can be seen ahead. Our path curves down to the left. In half a mile by a barn, turn right and go steeply downhill.

Fortunately, this brings you out opposite the climb to Hod Hill, another Iron Age fort, later occupied by the Romans. It is now a beautiful nature reserve with myriads of chalk-loving flowers. At the ramparts, keep straight on over Hod Hill south-east for half a mile. You leave the nature reserve coming down on a tree-lined track. At the bottom, a clear fast stream, the River Iwerne, welcomes you. Bear right and follow it to Manor Road which leads to the church.

From Stourpaine church cross the bordering field and head south towards a raised abandoned railway line. Go underneath the bridge then cross to a substantial footbridge to an island in the River Stour. Keep to the left to cross another footbridge off the island and you reach converted mill buildings. The track in front of the mill leads to A357. Turn left then right into the road diagonally opposite. This leads up through Durweston. At the next road junction in 100 metres, turn right then left for Durweston church.

The road past Durweston church is signposted to Bryanston. Walk south-west for one mile along this road then into Bryanston estate at an entrance marked 'Private'. This is a public footpath past the lodge on the right. The driveway to the school continues straight on but we turn right in 100 metres after the lodge. The footpath goes up through woodland, bearing left to the top of the hill. Turn right at the top and go behind school buildings. Turn left then right to make a loop then pass through a small residential area. The imposing main building can be seen on the left. Norman Shaw built it in 1890 for the second Viscount Portman. Cross the drive, go through a gate and cross a field diagonally to rejoin the drive at a building on the left.

Turn left then immediately right to the centre of Bryanston village. Walk up past the village shop, past a road to the left and past the club on the left.

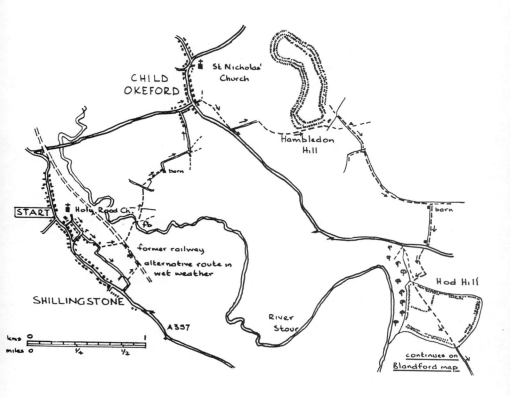

At the top go through a gate and cross a field diagonally left to rejoin the road. Turn right, follow the road past woodland and houses to the end. At T-junction with New Road outside the estate, turn left and follow the wall downhill. In half a mile turn left again along the pavement and past the grand entrance to the estate. Go across the bridge over the River Stour into Blandford Forum. The fine Georgian church is in Market Place.

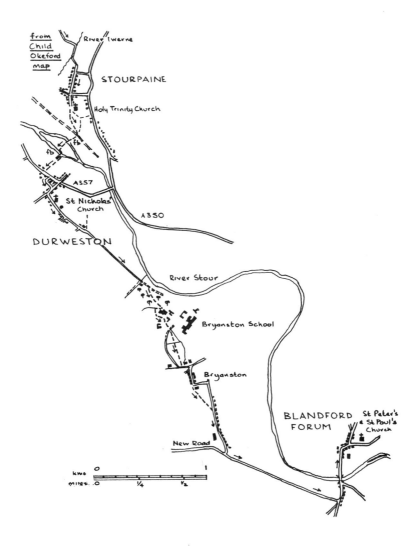

Walk 2

Almer – Mapperton – Winterborne Zelston – Winterborne Tomson – Anderson

Walking through lanes and across fields, we visit quiet villages and churches in the heart of Dorset. One of the churches is a perfect gem.

Starting point: Almer church, west of Wimborne Minster. GR913989
Maps: Explorer 118 and Landranger 194, 195
Distance: 6 miles
Terrain: flat

The Churches

St Mary, Almer, is an ancient church near the Elizabethan Almer Manor. The nave is Saxon in origin and there are Norman arches. The south doorway is also Norman. The chancel north window has a medley of stained glass, some of it Swiss. The tower is 15th century and the chancel Victorian. The shaft of a medieval preaching cross stands near the church. The little hamlet of Almer is outside the seven-mile wall, which excludes the public from Charborough Park.

St Andrew's at Winterborne Tomson, is built of flint, lime mortar and mixed stones and is a perfect Norman church. It has the only curved apse in Dorset. The plastered wagon roof has oak beams which curve over the sin-

St Andrew's at Winterborne Tomson is a Norman jewel just north of the A31, 4 miles from Bere Regis

gle cell building and follow the shape of the apse. The 18th-century oak pews are bleached white with age. The church was carefully restored to its early beauty in 1936 and is now in the care of the Churches Conservation Trust. The nearby 17th-century farmhouse is of brown stone rubble on the north side.

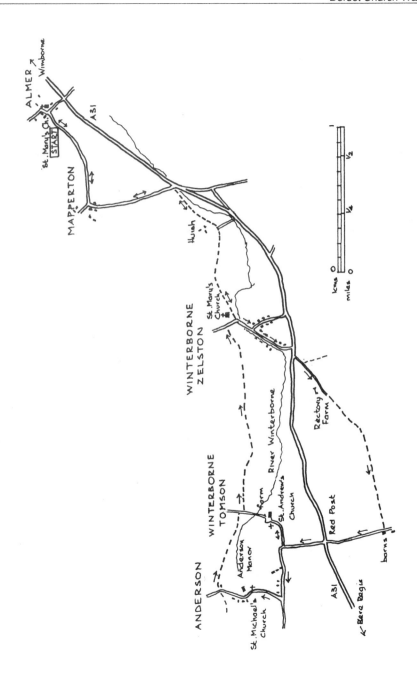

St Michael, Anderson, is a redundant chapel of flint with bands of carstone. It stands close to the handsome early 17th-century manor of red brick and white limestone.

St Mary's at Winterborne Zelston is a flint and brown stone streaked church, close to the fast-flowing stream. On the other side are thatched cottages and you may want to linger on the hump bridge as you cross over to them. The church itself has a Perpendicular tower. The rest is Victorian.

The Walk

From Almer church walk west along the hedge-lined lane to Mapperton, another hamlet about 300 metres away. Avoid the no through road on the right. Instead, follow the curve of the road to the left. Just before the main A31, turn right and continue west on a footpath across fields with a stream on the left. In 150 metres pass houses at Huish with an access road on the left.

The footpath carries on across fields, passing a wildlife pond on the right, then Winterborne Zelston church also on the right. Turn left at the village lane with houses facing the green and the Winterborne running alongside. Ignore the road on the left and walk past the medieval cross and bench on the right. Continue up to the A31 and cross with care to the footpath opposite on the right. Head south-west along a tarmac farm road. Avoid the path to the left and pass Rectory Farm on the right. The lane becomes a track and then a path across fields. At first there is a hedge on the left. Soon you see barns ahead. Go through a gap to the next field and now the hedge is on the right. Make for the barns and turn right onto the tarmac road. Cross the A31 again to the lane opposite. In 150 metres you come to the drive to Winterborne Tomson on the right. The Norman church and early 17th-century farmhouse stand on either side of the drive.

From Winterborne Tomson return along the drive to the entrance and carry on west to Anderson. Pass the driveway to Anderson Manor on the right. In another 100 metres, turn right up to Anderson church, a redundant Victorian chapel. The red brick manor is behind.

From Anderson chapel continue along the farm track and pass the manor on your right. At the first field entrance turn right and head east across the field. At a crossways turn right then left and walk along a tarmac lane for 200 metres. At farm buildings, the path kinks to the right before continuing east across fields. Below on your right you hear the traffic on A31. In 1 mile you cross the lane at Winterborne Zelston again, to visit a restored, conventional church.

From Winterborne Zelston return on the path along the edge of the churchyard, pass the wildlife pond, skirt around Huish and retrace your steps to Mapperton and Almer.

Walk 3

Milton Abbas – Winterborne Clenston
– Winterborne Stickland – Winterborne Houghton

From the pretty, purpose built village of Milton Abbas climb up to open fields and down through woodland to see villages which have grown naturally along the course of the Winterborne. (Milton Abbas can also be visited on Walk 14, Dorchester Section). Refreshments can be had at Winterborne Stickland village shop and pub.

Starting point: Milton Abbas church, parking on the road. GR805018
Maps: Explorer 117, Landranger 194
Distance: 10 miles
Terrain: hilly

The Churches

Visitors to the famous village of Milton Abbas often call in to view the church of Saint James. Joseph Damer, who bought Milton Abbey Estate in 1752, demolished the market town which had grown up around the Abbey. He was kind enough to house the workmen and women in a purpose-built village of small thatched houses, Milton Abbas. By chance the new village has a setting to appeal to today's visitors; a wooded slope down to an artificial lake with genuine 18th-century cottages lining the road. A new church was also provided and dedicated in 1786. It is a red sandstone building, originally Georgian Gothic. In 1888 a new chancel and south aisle were added. In 1969, the east window was fitted with glass designed by Laurence Lee.

St Nicholas, Winterborne Clenston, was built of flint and stone in 1840 with a slender broach spire. It has transepts but no aisles. This slim neat church stands alone in a narrow part of the Winterborne Valley. The Tudor Manor to the north seems remote from the church.

St Mary's, at Winterborne Stickland, was built of flint in 13th century. The 15th-century tower was built of bands of flint and stone. Both nave and chancel have wagon roofs. The fine chancel roof is painted in the bright colours favoured in the Middle Ages. There is a fine oak frame at the entrance to the Skinner Chapel. The Chapter of Coutances in Normandy held the manor here 1312-1341. 'Stikel-land is the Saxon name for 'steep land' and the 500-foot hill to the east now has a radio mast on top. At the crossroads outside the church, the remains of the Medieval Village Cross has been mounted on a block of Purbeck stone.

St Andrew's, in Winterborne Houghton, is an Early English flint church. The short tower is Perpendicular and the windows have been changed to that more ornate style. To the north on Meriden Down is an extensive Celtic field system.

The Walk

Face Milton Abbas church and take the footpath just to the left. Climb up through trees on a short steep slope to a field. Cross the field for 150 metres and turn left to walk along the field boundary. In 200 metres at a junction, turn right and you are on Jubilee Trail which you leave in 250 metres by turning left at a farm track. This takes you past riding stables down to a tarmac road.

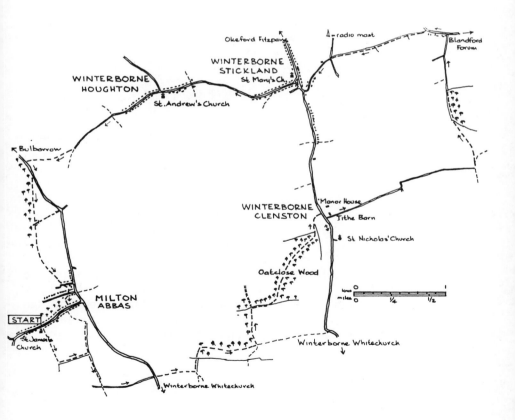

Cross to the path opposite, continue on course and turn left at a T-junction of paths. Walk down the field edge into woodland where the track is muddy at first. At a woodland opening turn right and keep straight on. In 250 metres turn left away from the main track. There is open ground on the right. Keep to the edge of the wood then turn right up a steep path with woods on the left and into Oatclose Wood. In half a mile this path brings you down to Winterborne Clenston at the Manor House. Turn right for the church, passing ancient barns.

From Winterborne Clenston church return to the tiled barn, turn right and walk up a farm track for over half a mile. Go under the power line, through a thick hedge and turn left along an elevated path with views east. Enter a welcome strip of trees and enjoy their protection for 250 metres. Emerge to join a tarmac farm road which takes you straight on until you reach a public road. Turn left and pass a campsite on the left. The road bends to the right and you go through a gate on the left and follow the field edge down to join the lane to Winterborne Stickland. The church is on the right. A shop and a pub are also in this village.

The lane in front of Winterborne Stickland church is signposted to Winterborne Houghton. Follow this quiet stream-lined lane up to the last of the Winterbornes.

After visiting Winterborne Houghton church avoid the road opposite to Bulbarrow and carry on through houses. In 380 metres ignore the bridleway on the right to Ibberton. Continue up the steep, hedge-lined track ahead to a farm gate opening onto downland. Take the raised path to the right through scattered trees with wonderful views to the right. When you see another gate ahead, do not go through it but veer left to the nearby tarmac road.

Turn left and walk along the road for 75 metres. Forestry Commission Land is on your right. At a gap and a notice board, the bridleway is clearly indicated. Keep woodland on your right as you head south for nearly a mile on the bridleway. On the way, pass a corrugated shack on the left, then a paddock, go round the edge of a tennis court to come out at the access road to a lodge. Turn right then left and cross a field with fine views south to Purbeck. You come to houses with a surgery on the left. Cross diagonally left, pass a playground to reach more houses. Follow the Jubilee Trail sign down through steps in woodland and continue down the path to Milton Abbas with church, post office, pub and teashops.

Walk 4

Ibberton Hill – Turnworth – Cross Dyke – Woolland

This walk starts high on the Wessex Ridgeway and descends South Down gently to reach a church which holds memories of Thomas Hardy. Either take the direct route back to the Ridgeway or spend a pleasant extra hour exploring a hidden valley and climbing to Iron Age and Roman earthworks at Ringmoor. Return to Wessex Ridgeway then descend to the west to a remote hamlet and church and climb back up to the car park at the picnic place, Ibberton Hill.

Starting point: Picnic Site, Ibberton Hill. GR791070

Maps: Explorer 117 and Landranger 194

Distance: 7 miles + 1 mile optional extra to Ringmoor

Terrain: Hilly

The Churches

The church of Saint Mary in Turnworth was Early English with a graceful flint and stone tower, added in the late 13th century. The rest of the church was rebuilt in 1869 in Gothic style. The newly qualified architect, Thomas Hardy, designed the capitals with early Gothic foliage. Twenty years later, as an author, he would cycle from Dorchester to read the lesson in this church where his friend, Thomas Perkins was Rector. The Revd. Perkins believed in justice to animals. Hardy described the village as 'lying in a hole, a narrow cleft beneath wooded slopes of Shillingstone Hill and Bell Hill'.

For Ibberton church, see Walk 5.

Woolland church was built in 1857 in Decorated style. Stones from the older building of 1547 were used in the new. It has a bell turret and slender spire. There is fine rib vaulting in the chancel and polygonal apse. The capitals have fine foliage. This little hamlet is overshaddowed by Bulbarrow and Ibberton Hill.

The Walk

Stay on the picnic site side of the road and go east along a high track between hedges. This track opens onto South Down. Keep the wire fence on your right and descend gently east towards Pleck Farm. In half a mile at the bottom, ignore the path on the left and bear right to walk along the valley. At crosspaths just before the farm, turn left. This is a bridleway which goes steeply uphill with thin woodland on the right. In 200 metres turn right and

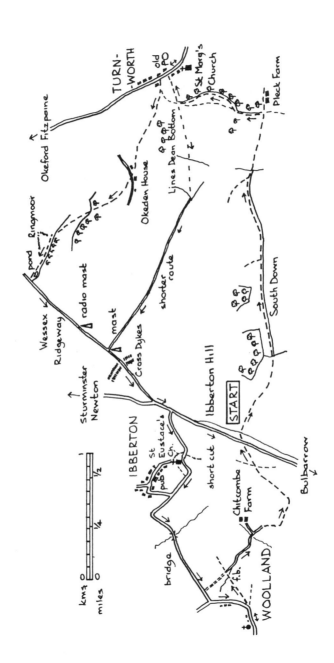

follow the track past strips of woodland on the right. (The line of the path is actually across the field, which may be ploughed. See map.)

In less than half a mile at a T-junction, you can see houses below on the right. Turn right and follow the little path down between hedges to Turnworth. The church is 100 metres on the right.

The shorter route: From Turnworth church, return to the footpath which brought you here and climb back up to the T-junction. Instead of turning left, keep straight on heading west uphill towards a magnificent tree. Down on your right are more trees in Lines Dean Bottom. At cross track keep straight on up across the open field to a corner where the hedge-rows meet. Veer right at this corner and the radio mast up on Cross Dyke can be seen ahead. Take the enclosed track up to Cross Dyke.

The longer route: This passes through some lovely remote countryside. From Turnworth church go back past the first footpath and past the old post office across the road on your right. Turn left onto a bridleway with a cottage on the right. Do not pursue the bridleway but turn right after the cottage and climb up through trees to the hedge. Follow the hedge, keeping it on your right, until you find the way through to the next field. Go through and head north-west passing through scattered trees. In 250 metres the buildings of Home Farm should come into view in the valley below. Go steeply down to the private tarmac road, passing a large barn at the bottom.

At Okeden House cross the road and follow footpath arrows uphill to woodland. In 300 metres the woodland curves left and you veer half-right on a grassy track across a rough field to the hedge boundary. Turn left and follow the hedge until you reach the bridleway access, marked with blue arrows, into Ringmoor earthworks on the right. These are owned by the National Trust. Cross the earthworks and turn left to the exit gate near a pond. The path passes the pond and emerges onto the Wessex Ridgeway. Turn left and Cross Dyke is 250 metres away. Here you join the shorter walk.

Both routes: head south-west along Wessex Ridgeway. In 250 metres you reach the tarmac road on Ibberton Hill. Turn left to walk along the road. *Keep heading south on the road if you wish to shorten the walk and return to the picnic place.*

To visit Ibberton and Woolland, turn right after 150 metres and take the steep lane marked to Ibberton. Descend through a tree canopy to the wide plain below. The village church and pub, which are also included in walk 5, are on the right. You can bypass them by keeping straight on and ignoring the turnings to the right. At the bottom our tarmac lane bends left and heads south-west between hedges for half a mile. Ignore all turnings until you reach a T-junction. Woolland is signposted to the left. Turn left for the church and note the footpath on the left in 250 metres. The church is 50 metres further along.

Woolland church is a pretty Victorian building at the foot of Bulbarrow Hill

From Woolland church re-
trace your steps for 50 metres
to the footpath, now on your
right. Go through a swing gate
into a young copse. The path
goes through the left side of
this copse and emerges at
rough common land. Follow
waymarkers to a narrow footbridge over a stream then to a
slender tarmac lane. Turn
right and follow the lane past a
bungalow and stables. Cross a
stream via a little bridge near
Chitcombe Farm. The
bridleway to Turnworth is
waymarked to the right. Follow it uphill with branches
overhead and mud in places
under foot. The way veers left
and comes up to downland.
Continue uphill heading
north-east and go through a
gate to the road at Ibberton Hill
Picnic Site.

Walk 5

Okeford Hill Picnic Site – Ibberton – Belchalwell – Okeford Fitzpaine

From the heights of the Wessex Ridgeway you plunge down to the hidden village of Ibberton. Walk across lanes and fields to the hamlet of Belchalwell whose church graces a lonely hillock. From there cross fields to Okeford Fitzpaine with its shop, pub and church. Climb gently back to the picnic site and enjoy the views to the hills in the east. Refreshments can be had at Ibberton Pub or Okeford Fitzpaine village stores.

Starting point: Okeford Hill Picnic Site on the Winterborne Road; GR812094

Maps: Explorer 117 and 129 Landranger194

Distance: 7 miles

Terrain: 1 steep slope downhill, 1 uphill, otherwise undulating

The Churches

St Eustace stands high above the village of Ibberton, looking out to Blackmoor Vale. It is a delightful, rural church. St Eustachius was a canonized Roman general. Was there a Roman influence in Ibberton once? There would appear to have been some Norman activity for the chancel contains memorial tablets to the D'aubeny brothers whose ancestors came to these shores with William The Conqueror. In more recent years the mainly Perpendicular church needed urgent repair and was rebuilt 1907-9. There is still some 15th-century glass in several windows and an Elizabethan oval in a north window. On the porch floor are 15th-century tiles with Flemish writing which translated advises:

> "The time is short
> Death is swift
> Guard against sin
> Then thou doest well".

At Belchalwell, St Aldhelm's is another dramatically sited church with views to Bulbarrow on one side and Blackmoor Vale on the other. 'Belchalwell' is Saxon for 'the hill by the cold stream'. The Norman origins of the church are clearly seen inside the porch; the doorway arch has zig-zag and dogtooth mouldings. The porch is set at an angle into the tower. A gargoyle on one corner of the tower is of a horned sheep. Puritans destroyed much of the interior of the church but there is a handsome Elizabethan pulpit.

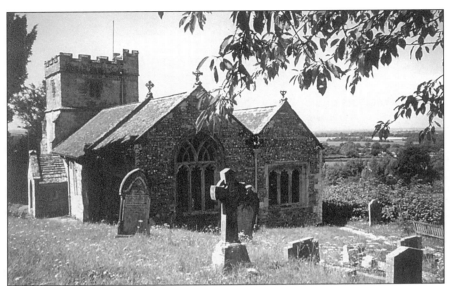

Ibberton church has a magnificent position overlooking Blackmoor Vale. The little village of Ibberton nestles below the church

Okeford Fitzpaine, St Andrew. It is hard to imagine a more perfect picture of a village than that of the view down the High Street and up to the church. This was rebuilt in 1866 using stones of the old building and copying its late medieval predecessor in Perpendicular style. Most of the interior is Victorian. There is a fine stone pulpit. One of the bells has the inscription:

'I often have been beate and banged
My friends rejoice to see me hanged
And when my friends do chance to die
Then I for them will loudly crie.'

The Walk

From the picnic site turn away from the road and head south-west along a clearly defined, elevated track for about one mile and a half. This is part of the Wessex Ridgeway, a long distance footpath. In half a mile you pass a pond in National Trust land on the left. In another half a mile pass the aerial at Cross Dyke before you start to descend towards Ibberton. Turn left at the road and walk for 150 metres. The first turning to the right is a steeply descending lane thickly overshadowed by trees. Go down here and take the first footpath off to the right to visit Ibberton church, high above the village. It is separated from the village by being on a slope too steep for traffic.

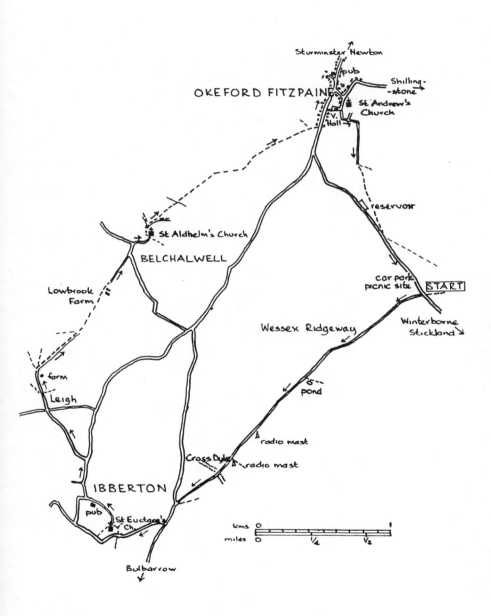

Leave Ibberton church by the gate on the east side and turn left to go down a farm track to the village. After the pub on the left you reach a T-junction and turn right towards Okeford Fitzpaine. At the first road on the left, turn left to Leigh. Keep straight on at crossroads. At the end of the lane there is a farm gate with arrows. Turn right and take the path with the hedge on your right. Lowbrook Farm and Belchalwell church beyond can be seen ahead. In half a mile go through the farmyard on the track which leads up to Belchalwell. At the village turn left then right up to the church which stands on a mound surveying the countryside for miles around.

From the gate of Belchalwell church, face the village and turn right on a footpath which goes behind the church and head north-east. Okeford Fitzpaine can be seen ahead. Follow arrows on gateposts and cross fields in a north–east course for over half a mile. Turn left when you reach the tarmac road at Okeford Fitzpaine and walk into the village. At crossroads the pub is straight on but we turn right, passing the village shop and post office. The church ahead has a most picturesque frame of white thatched cottages in front.

Turn right and walk up the lane in front of Okeford Fitzpaine church to the village hall. Find the footpath in the corner ahead. This bends left then right, becoming a track which climbs steadily between hedges. Views open to the left to Hambledon Hill and Hod Hill. Keep to the left of the reservoir, ignore the path to the left and make for the tarmac road to the right. Turn left on the road and go uphill for 200 metres and you are back at the picnic site.

Winterbourne Steepleton has one of only three
medieval spires in Dorset. (Walk 10)

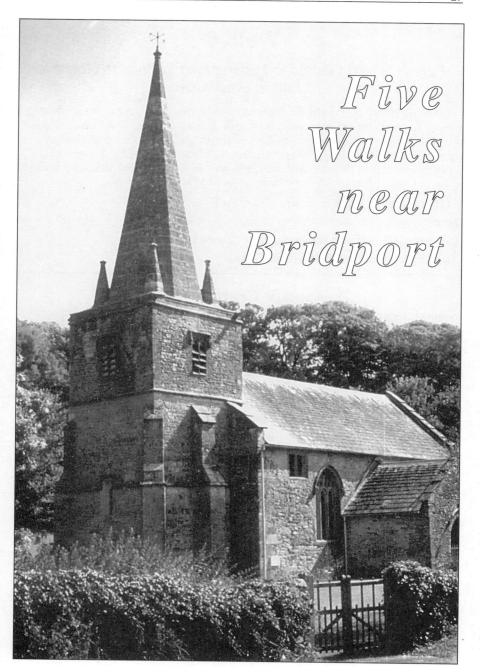

Five Walks near Bridport

Walk 6

Part 1: Shipton Gorge to Loders; **Part 2:** Shipton Gorge to
Burton Bradstock

*This walk offers you a choice. You may chose to walk inland from Shipton
Gorge to the pretty village of Loders with its exceptionally fine church. You
may prefer to head south to Burton Bradstock with a National Trust
restaurant overlooking the sea and walk along gentle cliffs to explore the
nature reserve at Cogden Beach. Each part has it share of hills and lanes.
Energetic walkers may want to try both parts.*

Starting point: Shipton Gorge church; GR498915

Maps: Outdoor Leisure 15 and Landranger 193, 194

Distances: Each part 6 miles – total 12 miles

Terrain: varied; hills, lanes, fields, coast

The Churches

Shipton Gorge, St Martin. There is no gorge here, only a church prettily
placed on a terrace above the village. The view south over coastal hills and
fields is extensive. In Domesday, Shipton was known as Sepetone. It belonged to the crown until 1260 AD. It passed to Thomas Maureward and became Shipton Maureward. Then the Norman family, de Gorges held it and
it became Shipton Gorges. The de Gorges family lost the estate in 1461. Although other distinguished families have held the estate, still the name
'Gorge' remains. St Martin was rebuilt and enlarged in 1862, apart from the
tower. The architect, J. Hicks once had Thomas Hardy as a pupil. The font
in Purbeck marble is 13th century.

Loders, St Mary Magdalene has a long history. This delightful church in
the walled garden close to the manor house, Loders Court, would have
started life as a parochial church linked to the manor. Go through the
church porch to see opposite the blocked Saxon north doorway. A Norman
doorway and window have survived in the mainly Early English chancel.
The nave walls are 14th century. In the north wall is a unique set of doors,
one above each other. These doorways lay hidden under plaster until an
1899 restoration. Also uncovered was a tombstone to the French monk,
Dom John Sampson, Prior in Loders in 1363. A group of monks had come to
Loders from France in 12th century at the invitation of the lord of the manor.
The chancel was their priory church and the nave stayed with the parish. In
1325, Edward I took away French dependencies in England. Henry IV restored them and the monks at Loders celebrated by building the Lady Cha-

Loders has a lovely old church in this stone village near Bridport

pel. This was in the new Perpendicular style. Also Perpendicular are the tower, the south aisle and south porch. This is two storey; a spiral stairway leads from the Lady Chapel to the priest's room above the porch.

Burton Bradstock, St Mary is built of local rubble stone, inferior Oolite and Forest Marble from Bothenhampton quarries. The pretty village has many houses of the same yellow-brown limestone. The River Bride runs through the village and has given the name 'Brideton', now Burton. 'Bradstock' harks back to the days when Bradenstoke Priory in Wiltshire owned land here. The church is mainly 15th century with gargoyles outside. It has retained the original cross shape of an earlier church. There are several square headed windows. In 1897 the south aisle was added.

The Walks

Part 1

From Shipton Gorge church go down to the village road and turn right. In 150 metres at crossways turn left into a lane signposted to Loders. Ignore paths to right and left. In 200 metres turn right at a road junction. The first half mile is along Loders Lane, the second half mile Shipton Lane. Shipton Hill on the right is a Bronze Age site. The lane goes down under the A35. Turn left as soon as you surface and go uphill for less than half a mile on a tarmac road with the A35, heard but not seen on the left. Ignore a path off to the right and turn right up a hedge-lined farm track over Knowl Hill to

Loders one mile away. From the top the church and village can be glimpsed down on the left. There is a bend in the lane to left and right. Then the real descent begins. At the tarmac lane at the bottom, turn left and follow its twisting course through the village. The little River Asker is beside you most of the way. The church is at the far western end. Once you reach the pub on the left, you have not much further to go for the church.

From Loders church, return towards the village and turn right almost immediately. A footpath takes you down to cross two footbridges, first over the mill stream, then over little River Asker. Boarsbarrow Hill looms ahead but we turn right and cross the meadow diagonally to Boarsbarrow Farm. Turn left here but do not go up the steep hill. Instead, take the track half-right, heading south and rising gently.

In half a mile, you reach the A35, which you cross diagonally to the right and find the turning to Walditch. Follow the road to the village (you may prefer the marked footpath if this is open). On the road, you pass a turning to the left. In about 150 metres, between cottages on the left, is a path marked to Shipton Gorge. Follow this sunken way uphill as far as you can. It emerges onto downland with strip lynchets on the right. There is also a quarry that would have provided stone for many local houses.

Keep on course with occasional hedgerow on the left. When you reach a cross hedgerow, you are at a T-junction of paths. Turn left and walk along the track with the hedge on your right. Turn to admire the distant view. A closer view can be had over a steep hollow below on the left with two isolated cottages. Ahead there are cottages at our level. Go through a farm gate and ignore the track on the left to the upper cottages. Avoid also the main enclosed track ahead. Instead, look for the footpath through a gap in the hedge opposite. This crosses the field diagonally south-east and enters Burbitt Lane, a farm track.

Turn left and follow the track down to Shipton Gorge, seen ahead. At the tarmac road, cross to Port Road opposite and walk down to a junction in the village. The church is high up on the right.

Part 2

From Shipton Gorge church, go down to the village road and turn left. At a T-junction, cross to the track opposite. There is an advertisement to New Inn next to this track. Walk up the track for about 100 metres and turn left over a stile. (There are many more stiles to come). Cross the field keeping fairly close to the boundary on the left. Continue across the middle of the next field and turn to look back at Shipton Gorge below. At the third field, keep more to the right. The fourth field is larger and you head up to the centre of the far boundary. In the fifth field climb diagonally right to a farm gate. Go through the gate to Milvers Lane, a rough track and turn left.

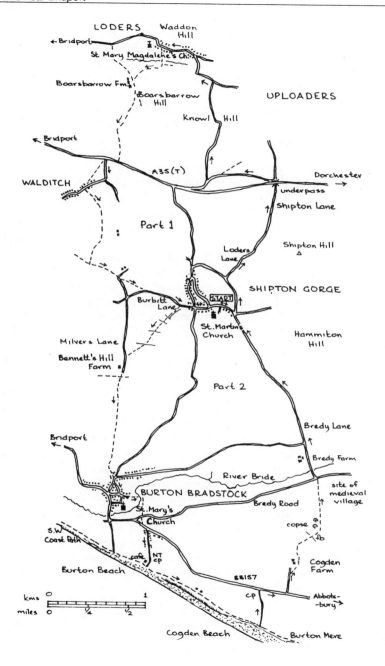

Walk up Milvers Lane to the end. Cross diagonally right to a footpath which heads south down an open field. The path ascends then descends and reaches a wide new track down to Burton Bradstock. When you reach the road, turn right and go south through golden stone cottages to the church.

From Burton Bradstock church, go past the village school next door. Cross the bridge over the little River Bride and then follow the footpath signs to the beach. The path goes south past a caravan site, crosses two roads then turns down Beach Road and through a car park to the sea. The National Trust teashop welcomes you here unless the weather is very bad or it is Christmas! It opens at 10 am and may close early in the winter. Tasty meals and snacks are served.

From the National Trust Teashop face the sea and turn left. Follow the South West Coastal Path climbing south-east over moderate cliffs. Walk below a caravan site and down to the wide expanse of Cogden Beach. This is a nature reserve with Burton Mere ahead. Just before the mere, at one of the two lifebelt stations, turn left and follow one of the tracks, both leading up to the National Trust Car Park at the B3157.

Turn right and walk carefully along the verge of this busy road for 200 metres then cross to Cogden Farm opposite. *Look out for a possible future path inside National Trust land and leading to this road crossing to Cogden Farm.*

The footpath sign on the main road is clear, but not at the farm. Walk towards the farm until the track forks. Take the right fork towards a house called 'Chesil' and go through the farm gate near this house. Cross to a barn and join a track leading away north from the farm. Climb the track until you have a view of Burton Bradstock down to the left.

Look across to a copse about 200 metres away to the right. You have to head for the right-hand edge of the copse. You go down to cross a narrow watercourse then up to the copse. On the right there are parallel bars to climb into the next field. On the other side it is a delight to find the farmer has cleared a wide footpath. Follow the hedge on your left down to the Bredy Road. The medieval village of Modbury once stood to the east of our path. There is some evidence of it on the north side of the road.

Cross Bredy Road diagonally left and go up Bredy Lane, passing Bredy Farm. As this is a quiet lane, you can follow it for one and a half miles to Shipton Gorge. (There is a field route if you turn left after Bredy Farm but it tends to be waterlogged in wet weather). To continue on the road way up to Shipton Gorge, you pass Cathole Farm and Hammiton Hill on your right. This is the oldest local archaeological site with Bronze Age barrows. At a crossroads, turn left for Shipton Gorge. At a road junction in the village, turn left and climb back up to the church.

Walk 7

Charmouth — Wootton Fitzpaine and then to Lyme Regis or Catherston Leweston

Again you have a choice of walks, both with spectacular views from hills into wooded valleys with streams and rivulets. The longer walk also touches the coast.

Starting point: Charmouth Post Office GR365936

Maps: Explorer 116 and Landranger 193

Distances: 10 or 5½ miles

Terrain: Gentle hills

Warning note

The longer walk to Lyme Regis, following Liberty Trail and Wessex Ridgeway, has to cross the A35 on Penn Hill where the traffic is moving fast. I am pressing The Highways Agency, Falcon Road, Exeter to make some concession to pedestrians here. If you have doubts, I suggest you follow the shorter walk. Then take a 31 bus to Lyme (hourly service, Sunday less frequent) and walk back.

The Churches

St Andrew's, Charmouth, is a Victorian church designed by Charles Fowler. It contains a 15th-century statuette of an abbot against a cross. Charmouth once belonged to Forde Abbey. Thomas Chard, the last abbot of Forde almost certainly stayed at The Queen's Arms in the High Street. The inn consists of two Tudor houses joined together. Jane Austen enjoyed 'quiet contemplation' of the hills, cliffs and sea views of Charmouth.

Wootton Fitzpaine church is set in a quiet wooded and hilly part of Dorset. It is close to Wootton House and surrounded by trees. Wootton House, was built in 1765 and enlarged in 1896. The church, in the shape of a cross has been much restored by the Victorians. The tower has Early English arches, the chancel is Decorated and the south chapel is Perpendicular.

St Michael's is the parish church of this hilly seaside town of Lyme Regis. The church is built of blue lias stone, not the best choice for a building on an exposed cliff site. Blue lias is a soft stone and the walls have had to be repeatedly repaired. In Saxon days there was more land between the church and the sea. The church then was more sheltered. Land has since eroded. The present building houses two churches. The old Norman

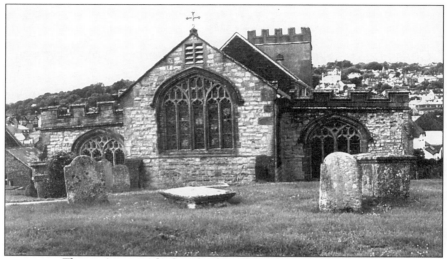

The ancient parish church of Lyme Regis overlooks the sea

church serves as a huge porch to the later Perpendicular building with its wide nave and aisles with six bays. The west tower was once the central tower of the Norman church. The lower part of the tower is even older; a Saxon window has recently been discovered in the south wall. In 774 AD Cynewulf, King of the West Saxons, granted land in Lyme to Sherborne Abbey. Salt for food preservation was extracted by boiling sea water. In the 13th century an artificial harbour, the Cobb was built. It is a great curving wall which made Lyme into a busy port until the 17th century when ships were too big to enter the harbour. The Cobb still stands, a monument to those medieval builders and masons.

Catherston Leweston church was built in 1857 and was commissioned by Mr. Charles Hildyard QC, MP whose only son was killed in a shooting accident in 1876. They are both interred behind the church. The stonework of the little church is an unusual pattern of smooth pinky grey, white and beige cobs of chert. Here is a sad and pretty place among trees.

The Walks

Both parts:

From Charmouth Post Office head north past the recreation ground and along Monarch's Way, a long distance path. This passes under the A35 and crosses fields going gradually uphill in a gentle valley. There is a brook on the right. Keep on route for about half a mile, crossing two footbridges. After the second footbridge, walk up the incline towards the hedge. Monarchs Way goes to the left. A house can be seen ahead to the right. You go to the right keeping the hedge away to the left. You come out at a tarmac lane with the house on your left. Cross to the footpath opposite. The village of Wootton Fitzpaine, some distance from the church, can be seen across the field to the left. Cross one field diagonally left and go over a footbridge to the next field where you cut across the left-hand corner. In the third field, turn right. In 300 metres you reach the driveway of Wootton House. Turn left on the driveway and go up to Wootton Lane. Turn right and the church is 100 metres along this lane on the right.

The longer walk to Lyme Regis

From Wootton Fitzpaine church, retrace your steps along Wootton Lane. Pass Wootton House driveway and continue west along the lane to a T-junction in the village. Keep straight on for 250 metres heading west on the narrow Meerhay Lane.

If you want to keep dry feet, stay on the hedge-lined lane for one mile. Turn left just after a bridge, keep the hedge on your left and head for the big barn.

If you prefer adventure and fine views, turn left at Meerhay Farm. Go no further than the first farm building and turn right. There are arrows marking Liberty Trail and Wessex Ridgeway. We follow these long distance paths all the way to Lyme Regis. At first this is a bumpy route across fields with woodland on the left. Keep a sharp lookout for arrows indicating the trails. Pass an old stone cottage, then descend to a hollow with derelict farm buildings. Cross a babbling brook on a footbridge then follow the brook on your right to reach Stubbs Farm.

The Meerhay Lane walk joins here.

At Stubbs Farm go past the big barn and turn sharp left uphill with woodland on the left. In 100 metres near a pond, the path veers right to pass in front of a squat barn. Go through a gate and head uphill. Penn Farm can be seen up on the right. Pass the farm on the right and turn left at the farm road. This brings you to a layby with the A35 beyond.

The most direct way over the A35 is diagonally left to a tantalising road opposite, but it may be safer to find the central reservation higher up the A35, cross over and walk down the verge. When you reach the road, no longer tantalising, turn immediately right, following arrows.

Continue on Liberty Trail down towards thick woodland which you enter at the bottom. After we have gone 250 metres heading south-west in the wood, the trees give way. Avoid crossing the footbridge on the right into Devon. Head south and join a track for 50 metres. Turn left off this track and back into woodland following Liberty Trail south-east, then south, through conifers with some ash and sweet chestnuts.

Go through a ford and in 100 metres emerge from the wood at the driveway of a detached house. Make for the track which continues your southerly direction. In 250 metres at cross bridleways, turn right and a view opens down to the valley of the little River Lim and across to Uplyme. Go down open fields towards a sewage works which you pass on your left.

At the lane turn left, keeping to Wessex Ridgeway which follows the little River Lim for 1 mile into Lyme Regis. Cross a suburban road to Windsor Terrace, then along the riverside walk. Keep heading south-east to the sea. The famous Lyme Regis Cobb, an ancient sea wall is to the right. Our route is to the left, past the Information Centre to St Michael's Church.

From St Michael's Church continue up the main A3052. In 300 metres you can avoid some traffic by going through the car park on the right to the football ground. Charmouth is clearly indicated uphill across the fields. At the second field avoid the right-hand corner and the dreaded Spittles maze. Go left towards the main road. Then follow the coastal route, which climbs wooden steps up through steep woodland, goes round a hollow and straightens out at the top. It flanks the golf links and offers views to the sea and to the rocky coast beyond Charmouth.

Too soon the path starts descending on a narrow tarmac lane with occasional houses. The lane brings you to The Street, Charmouth. Turn right for the church and post office.

Shorter walk from Wootton Fitzpaine to Charmouth

From Wootton Fitzpaine church face the track opposite but avoid following the Wessex Ridgeway here. Instead turn right along Wootton Lane. Go past Manor Barn to the wide double gates of Manor Farm. Turn right and go through the farmyard between barns and keep on track to a stream shaded by trees. The track curves right behind Wootton church and House, crosses the stream and starts uphill on its concrete way. The official right of way is to the left of the concrete track, heading towards Conegar Hill then veering right. It rejoins the concrete track in less than half a mile at a higher point.

As you climb you realise you are walking round the edge of a large natural basin with delightful views. At a T-junction with finger posts, turn right and head south-west on the southern rim of the basin. Down to the right Wootton House stands serene. Keep the field boundary on your left and make for pine trees at the top. Pass a footpath on the left, then the pine trees.

You are heading for Catherston Leweston, a hamlet above Charmouth. Just as you approach a copse of beech trees, turn left onto a footpath across a field. Now the copse is on your right. Follow the well-worn way to a farm gate on the left, then into the next field, going downhill towards a barn.

Keep the barn well to the right and turn left to cross a stile next to the gate. There is then a short field crossing to the tarmac road. The bungalow on your right faces the road.

Climb down to the road and pass a wooden Jubilee seat on the left. Next you are at the entrance to Catherston Manor, built in 1887 in Early Tudor style. The church is 100 metres up the driveway and the manor, now private apartments can only be glimpsed.

From Catherston Leweston church return to the road, turn left and cross the bridge over the busy A35. Your road leads through caravan sites down to the eastern side of Charmouth. Turn right and walk back to the post office along The Street.

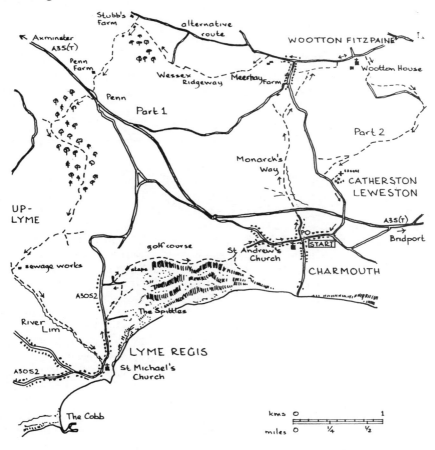

Walk 8

Symondsbury – Whitchurch Canonicorum (then optionally via St Gabriel and Golden Cap to Seatown)

Follow in the footsteps of pilgrims who have braved the threat of violent robbery and crossed uncharted land to seek healing at the shrine of St Wite since medieval times. We return to Symondsbury along a glorious, bracing part of the Dorset Coast with the chance of a dip in the sea at Seatown. This last part is quite strenuous and can be avoided by catching a bus at Morecombelake (see The Walk below).

Starting point: the 'no through road' beside Symondsbury church. GR445936

Maps: Explorer 116 and Landranger 193

Distances: 12 miles or 5 miles

Public transport: At the time of writing, bus 31 (First Southern National Tel: 01305 783645) provides an hourly service, less frequent Sunday. In addition there is an X53 bus and extra buses in the summer.

Terrain: undulating to hilly

The Churches

St John The Baptist, Symondsbury, is of golden brown local sandstone. This mainly 14th-and 15th-century church has an aura of a more distant past. The 14th-century tower is in the centre of the cruciform church. There are high stone arches and a waggon head barrel roof built in 15th century by shipwrights from West Bay. The porch, also 15th century has stayed unchanged. The rest of the church has suffered two reformations. The first early in 19th century aimed at eliminating the Gothic character; the second a counter reformation early in 20th century undid the work of the first. Fortunately, the Georgian altar rails and pulpit were unscathed.

Whitchurch Canonicorum: St Candida or St Wite. King Alfred left the church of 'Hwitancircian' to his youngest son, Ethelwald. Was the church called 'hwit' because it was built of stone, not wood, or because St Wita was the patron saint? St Wita may have been a kindly hermitess of eighth century, famous for her healing powers. Her bones are still in the stone shrine in the church. In medieval times, the disabled would thrust their ailing limbs into one of the three holes in the coffin. Even today, coins are thrown inside. They are collected and sent to causes aiding the sick. There are also letters to St Wite. Miraculously her shrine escaped both the Reformation and destruction by Cromwell's men. Yet this was an important church.

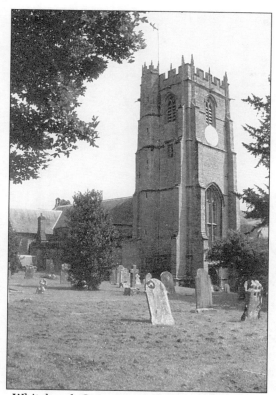

Whitchurch Canonicorum has an ancient and imposing church which reflects a glorious past

William the Conqueror mentioned it and 'Brideton' in a charter granting them to the Monastery of Fontanelle. The monks had difficulties in building the new Norman church to replace the Saxon one. At the end of the 12th century the Bishop of Sarum took over and built transepts, extended the chancel and rebuilt the arch. This is the same church standing here today. The tower and porch were added in the 14th century. The church was shared with canons from Salisbury and Wells, hence 'Canonicorum'. In Marchwood Vale all paths lead to Whitchurch Canonicorum. We are walking along ancient ways.

St Gabriel's, Stanton, is a lonely ruin on the beautiful coast near Golden Cap. In the 14th century it was a chapel to Whitchurch Canonicorum and there was a sizeable fishing village. Occasional outdoor plays are held here in the summer.

The Walk

From Symondsbury church go up the no through road heading west in a sunken lane. Higher up there are steep cliffs on either side. You are skirting high on Colmer Hill. In half a mile avoid the path on the right Keep on the enclosed lane past a lone thatched cottage on the right. At crossways at the top take the second turning left down Hell Lane. This is not as hostile as the name suggests. About half way down there is a view over to a lake on the right. Continue down and the track becomes a tarmac lane. Pass some cottages on the lane and bear left at the first junction.

Keep on course, north-west, along the edge of the quiet village of North

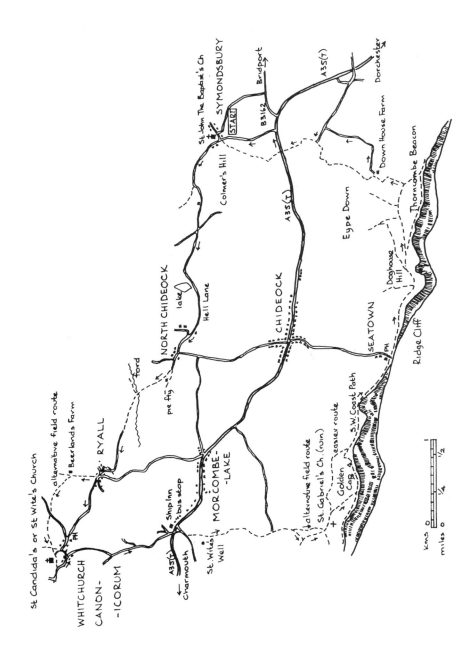

Chideock and avoid lanes to left and right. After half a mile of tarmac lane, you come to a farm track which continues in the same north-west direction. Avoid the footpath to the left and an unlikely pie factory, also on the left. Hedges and ferns are on either side of the track which leads to a little ford. Cross the stream and avoid the bridleway to the right. Keep straight on up a grassy track through farmland. Go past the pictureque cottage in a hollow on the left then turn right and walk along a track to the hamlet of Ryall.

Ryall is criss-crossed with lanes but if you keep heading north-west you should come to the tarmac road to Whitchurch Canonicorum. If in doubt, ask the way.

For the more adventurous there is a longer footpath way. As you leave Ryall at Hope Cottage, turn right down the farm drive to Beerlands Farm. Turn left across fields, pass a small lake and go downhill to a tarmac lane. Cross the lane to the footpath opposite (there is a stile next to the driveway of 'Blaney'). Follow the stream on your left. As you approach the church, cross the stile in the hedge on the left and turn right along a grassy track to the churchyard.

In half a mile the road walkers will pass a pub, the Five Bells, on the left. The church can be seen down the slope ahead. The footpath to the church is on the right in a corner of the road.

From Whitchurch Canonicorum church go down the front drive, turn left at the road and walk uphill. (It is uphill for nearly one mile now). In 150 metres the lane to the right is signposted to Morcombelake. Go up here to a T-junction and turn left. This lane leads through the village of Morcombelake to the A35. The Ship Inn and a bus stop are on your left. You can catch the 31 bus here. It passes the turning to Symondsbury on the way to Bridport.

For those wishing to return on the coastal route, cross the A35 to a narrow tarmac road opposite. In 50 metres, another road joins us from the left. Continue south-west along the old stage coach road for another 50 metres then turn left. The finger post to Golden Cap is hidden in the hedge. Keep on this track to Golden Cap for about one mile and avoid turnings to right and left. At the end there are National Trust holiday cottages. Turn left and you come to the sequestered ruin of St Gabriel's Church.

Continue on the path past St Gabriel's and into the next field. Cross diagonally to the signpost at the foot of Golden Cap. At 617 feet this is the highest cliff in the south of England. The sandy soil at the top gives the gold colour of its name. This is quite a steep climb on the Dorset Coast Path. (There is an easier way around Golden Cap and Brian Panton has marked it on the sketch map. Note: some diversions are not yet shown on O.S. Maps.)

For the climbers: keep on route to the trig. point with a glorious view along the coast to Seatown and Thorncombe Beacon beyond. The descent from Golden Cap is on the left of the trig. point. It goes inland and then immediately curves down to the right around Golden Cap on steps down to a kissing gate. Keep on the coastal path to the beach at Seatown.

Go through the beach car park then up the next cliff, Ridge Cliff. Then drop down to the signpost at the bottom of Doghouse Hill. You can go up this steep hill keeping the cliffs and Thorncombe Beacon on your right. *Before the climb up Doghouse Hill, it is possible to take the grassy path to the left and take a gentler route. Keep the hedge on your left until you come to a well-defined track rising towards Thorncombe Beacon on the right. Go up this track and turn left round an old post at the top. Head for a gate, stile and tumulus.* Keep Thorncombe Beacon on your right and ignore the path to Eype Down on the left. Instead, keep on the lower path and in about 250 metres at a gate on the left, turn left towards Down House Farm.

The footpath goes to the left of the farm. At crossways follow the lane signposted to Eype. In half a mile of narrow, tarmac lane, you reach a T-junction. Turn left and in 150 metres there is a path to the right. Take this path through trees and down a short steep hill to a wood. Cross a footbridge over a stream and turn left at the edge of a field, keeping the woodland on your left. The ground rises and you have to head for the hedge in front and find a gate in the corner. Climb over the stile and go up a track to a white house near the A35.

You have a choice of routes, both under half a mile, back to Symondsbury.

For the field way, cross the A35 diagonally to the right. Peer up driveways to find a gate with yellow arrows which show the way across delightful hilly countryside. Straight ahead you look across to Colmer's, a distinctive little hill, topped with 5 or 6 pine trees. Our route is downhill keeping quite close to the field hedge on the right. At the bottom cross a stream overhung with trees. Emerge to cross a narrow field to the gate and stile facing you. Once across, you skirt the hill slope at mid- level. Pass trees, including a magnificent sweet chestnut. Symondsbury church can be seen ahead. Go gently down to the left where you leave the field by a watery access track. The church is to your left and the pub to your right.

For the road way, cross the A35 and turn right to walk along the pavement beside the main road. This descends and is screened from traffic by trees and bushes. In 150 metres you reach the road to Symondsbury. Turn left along this road and you soon come to the pub on your right and the church ahead.

Walk 9

Netherbury – Beaminster – Stoke Abbott

A varied walk – Dorset villages at their loveliest, tiny rivers overhung with trees, hill climbs, secluded woods and valleys, a Tudor Mansion and perhaps the finest church tower in Dorset. Parnham House can be visited from April to October, Sundays, Wednesdays and Bank Holidays.

Starting point: The Village Hall, Netherbury; GR470995

Maps: Explorer 116 and Landranger 193

Distance: 6 miles.

Terrain: Varied, some hills, some muddy

The Churches

St Mary's has one of the finest towers in Dorset. Beaminster is a busy, lively place.

Netherbury's St Mary The Virgin stands on one of the many hills hereabouts. The walk up to the church from the yellow stone cottages of the village is enchanting. The high tower is Perpendicular but the porch was rebuilt in1848. Angels replaced gargoyles for corner carvings. Inside, the nave has 14th-century arcades and the chancel is 15th century. The battered alabaster tomb is mid-15th century. It may be an effigy of James More who was killed in the Wars of the Roses. There is a fine Jacobean pulpit. 'Niderburie' was an important church in 1086 when it belonged to the Bishopric of Sarum.

Beaminster's St Mary stands on what is probably a prehistoric sacred mound. 'Begaminster' takes its name from the Saxon Saint Bega

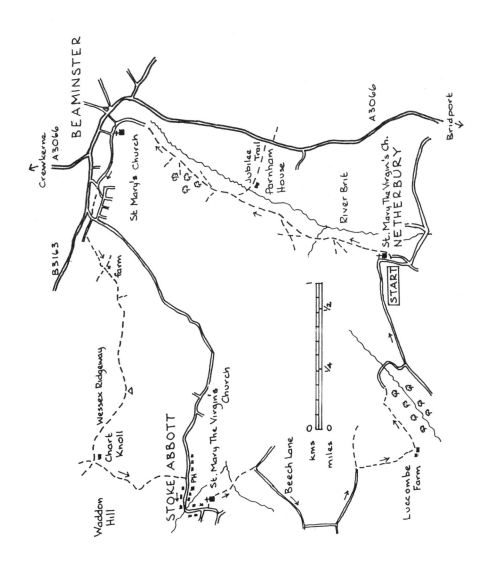

who may originally have been the patron saint here. The Norman church with a central tower was replaced in 15th century. The western arcading in the nave has vine sculpture on the capitals. The ceiling is Victorian and the supports for the beams are of Bath stone. The magnificent tower of 1500 AD has 41 pinnacles, each resting on a stone devil or mythical animal. In the north-west corner stands Saint Bega. Above her is King Alfred. Among the religious figures on the west face of the tower is a fuller, holding the tools of his craft in flax: a bat and a mill. Fortunately the church escaped the town fires of 1684 and 1781.

Another St Mary The Virgin is visited in Stoke Abbott. 'Stoche' in Domesday was held by the Bishop of Salisbury. From this Norman period there remains a small window in the north wall of the chancel and a beautifully carved font with eight heads, possibly Noah and his family. The chancel was lengthened in 13th century and the lancet windows are Early English. Stand in the chancel and look towards the bell tower. The shafts of light through the bell tower window illuminate the early 13th-century tower arch. The south wall of the nave is 13th century with two 15th-century windows. There is an interesting book, a Narrative of Life in Stoke Abbott at the turn of the century by Frederick Swaffield who came to live in the village in 1895. He mentions 'the blacksmiths, carpenters, carters, shepherds, cowmen, hurdlemakers, flaxdressers, rabbit catchers, farmers and all…village life seems full of beauty; people were poor but everybody seemed happy and everybody at work'. A copy of this narrative is in the County Archives. One survival from the past, the curfew is still rung in Stoke Abbott at 7 am in the summer. The thatched cottages of yellow limestone from nearby Waddon Hill are as lovely as ever.

The Walk

Climb up the narrow drive to the church. At the gates a slender path goes off to the right. After visiting the church take this path below the churchyard. Keep your eyes near the ground and at a path junction you will find arrows with captions marking Hardy Way and Brit Valley Way. We follow the Brit Valley waymarks north to Beaminster. The stream beside us on the right is the River Brit. Do not be tempted off to the left and keep to the path with woodland on the right. In about 300 metres pass Parnham House, a Tudor Mansion on the right, obscured by trees in summer. Just before a gate on our route, Jubilee Trail indicated to the right leads to Parnham House.

We continue north through Parnham Park. Brit Valley Way veers left to the next field. There are cottages ahead. Keep them on the right as you climb to the gap between a towering wooded hill and bordering trees. Keep close to the trees on the right and then join a hard track into Beaminster.

This track becomes St Mary Well Street. At the T-junction the church is on your left and the town square to the right.

From Beaminster church continue on the little lane below the church. This is part of the Wessex Ridgeway and goes through a residential part following the stream on the left. Then it crosses a meadow to a tarmac lane. *(Turn left and follow the lane for one mile if you want to avoid the hills.)*

For the more energetic, the Wessex Ridgeway crosses the lane and turns right into Half Acre Lane. Turn left opposite a row of houses and go up across fields towards the barns of Higher Barrowfield Farm. Pass the farm and make for the hills. First go down through a new tree plantation, cross a footbridge over a stream, then start climbing up Gerrard's Hill. Head for the beech trees and pass a triangulation point on the left. Continue for 300 metres to crosspaths at Chart Knolle. There are views to the many little hills around.

Turn left with a farm on the left and follow the path through woodland then down to the driveway and descend between high banks to Stoke Abbott about half a mile below. At the village lane turn right, passing the pub and a handsome manor farm in the corner where the road bends south. Pass a turning on the right and, in a few metres, the narrow drive to the church is on the left.

From Stoke Abbott church go behind the chancel and make for one of two muddy bridges over a stream below. The right-hand one by the hedge is the right of way. Once across, climb up 50 metres to a path in a sunken way between steep banks and high hedges. Go up this enclosed way for 100 metres. Just past a path on the left, the trees give way and you climb steeply up to an opening. Take the track on the right, Beech Lane which heads up south-west. You can see over the hedges on either side to the little hills around.

In less than half a mile turn left and walk due south on the track. In 200 metres at the top turn left on a concrete track for 250 metres. At the end of the concrete, the track continues but we turn right through a farm gate with the name 'Luccombe' on it.

Go along the path with a hedge on the right. When you see the farm below bear left and keep the farm on your right. When you are level with the farm building, turn left, go through a gap in a tall hedge and cross a field with woodland on the right. At the end of the field go down into the woodland with the stream below and continue on a muddy way. This veers right uphill and is enclosed with bracken and blackberry. Locals seem to have made an unofficial way to the left of the enclosed right of way. You emerge onto a track which swings right and then left to reach a tarmac road.

Turn left and walk along the road for about half a mile to Netherbury. The church welcomes you back to the village.

Walk 10

Winterbourne Steepleton – Hardy Monument – Portesham – Abbotsbury (– Little Bredy)

This is a long walk of great beauty and variety. After Hardy Monument, commemorating the sailor Hardy, we have glimpses of the sea and Chesil Beach. It is possible to shorten the walk after Abbotsbury by returning to the Hardy Monument on the South West Coast Path but then you would miss the idyllic village of Little Bredy.

Starting point: Winterbourne Steepleton church; GR618905
Maps: Outdoor Leisure 15 and Landranger 194
Distances: 12 or 10½ miles
Terrain: Hilly

The Churches

St Michael's in Winterbourne Steepleton has a 14th-century tower with a stone spire. The Archangel Michael is depicted in the lively Saxon carving of a flying angel. This may have been one of a pair and has been brought inside the church. There are fragments of medieval wall paintings in the nave. Most of the church is 12th to 13th century with a blocked Norman north door and a Norman font. Outside, the little river was in full flow in July 1999. There is a small row of grey stone cottages retiring behind the church. Less retiring is the bold 19th-century manor in Portland stone opposite. It is now a nursing home.

A church existed in Portesham in Saxon times. King Canute gave it to his steward, Orc in 1023 AD. Orc left it to Abbotsbury Abbey. The present building, St Peter's, has a 12th-century nave with a blocked Norman doorway in the north wall and a blocked arcade. The font is also Norman. Most of the remaining church, the chancel, aisles and tower were built around 1500 AD. The aisles are in line with the chancel, not the nave. There is an early 13th-century doorway with trefoil head in the north wall of the chancel. The churchyard has several interesting monuments including William Weare's epitaph on the church wall outside near the porch. His land may have been invaded by Roundheads in 1644. The sailor who shared Thomas Hardy's name lived at Portesham Manor. The village has several grey stone cottages.

In Abbotsbury, the parish church of St Nicholas stands between the Benedictine Abbey and the golden village of Abbotsbury. The abbey church, believed to date back to Roman times, was just south of the parish church. In 1044, Orc and his wife Thola founded the Benedictine monastery which thrived until the Dissolution. Now it is in ruin. The large tithe barn of 1400 is in better condition. One of the early abbots with staff and book has found refuge in the parish church porch. His stone effigy is here. Much of the church is Perpendicular but the north porch and north aisle are Decorated. The beautiful plaster barrel ceiling in the chancel is 17th century. The Jacobean pulpit has two bullet holes from the Civil War. Near Abbotsbury, prominent on a hill to the south, stands the 15th-century monastery chapel to St Catherine. Angels are said to have lifted her body to Mount Sinai after her death. This is a sturdy chapel with an unusual tunnel vault.

St Michael's, Little Bredy, is a Victorian church, topped with an attractive spire. Much of the charm of the village lies in its setting among hills rich in Bronze Age barrows and Celtic field systems.

The Walk

With your back to Winterbourne Steepleton church, turn right and go through the village for 150 metres. Turn left onto the bridleway signposted to Bronkham Hill. The track bends right then left and uphill. Broken hedge and two separate lines of trees are on the left as you plod uphill. Go under the line of pylons. Hardy Monument can be seen ahead. In half a mile the path curves left and there is a wood nearby on the right. Ahead is the tarmac road up to the monument.

When you reach the tarmac road, turn right and walk up it for 250 metres. A path off to the right, marked 'Inland Route' avoids the road. This is the inland route of the South West Coast Path. At the top it crosses the road and passes Hardy Monument on the left, then continues south-west. According to the marker on the ground, it is heading for West Bexington, six miles away on the coast. We only follow it for about half a mile.

First, admire the magnificent views from the monument (to T. Hardy, the sailor). Return to the marker and plunge south-west on the Coast Path. It descends through sand and bracken then continues down through woodland. Keep to the main path and avoid turnings. You emerge from the wood and turn left, leaving the South West Coast Path.

Our footpath is signposted to Portesham. In 50 metres there is a T-junction of paths near some barns. Turn right and follow the track uphill for 100 metres. Just before the top of the hill, turn right into farmland. Unusually there are stone walls here. Soon the village of Portesham can be seen below with a dramatic sweep of land and the sea beyond. To the right, the famous local landmark, St Catherine's Chapel comes into view on the hill.

You enter Portesham on the north side, turning left at the post office and walk down through the village. The brook follows the same route and

passes the pretty village church on the right. You come out on the south
side of Portesham and follow the road towards Abbotsbury. At the edge of
the village turn right onto a track signed 'Evershot Farms Ltd. Manor Dairy'.
At a fork in the track keep straight on along the old railway track heading
west. In about one mile you turn left and reach Abbotsbury. Turn right at
the road and cross to the pub, The Swan. You can walk through the pub
grounds to the Priory Car Park. The church is ahead; the Priory below on
the left.

From Abbotsbury church, go to the High Street (B3157) and turn right. In 75 metres turn left up Rosemary Lane. This leads to a T-junction. Turn right and continue uphill on a lane leading away from the village. Further up, it is called Bishop's Road. We leave it in 250 metres to turn left on a bridleway indicated to White Hill. This leads up past strip lynchets and joins the South West Coast Path at the top of the hill. Follow the Coast Path straight on and in 100 metres you rejoin Bishop's Road. Go up the road heading north-east.

It is possible to shorten the walk here by one mile: turn right and follow the South West Coast Path back to Hardy Monument and then retrace your steps to Winterbourne Steepleton.

For the full walk, continue up Bishop's Road for 75 metres and turn left on the tarmac access road to a camp site and Gorwell Farm. At a cattle grid take the right-hand track then turn sharp right, heading north. The track is stony with low fencing on either side. In half a mile, just before a farm building, go left off the track but keep close to the farm and woodland on your right.

On the open hill ahead, inviting tracks beckon. The official route follows the edge of the wood and becomes a wide grassy way above the delightful valleys and trees of parkland below. Reluctantly descend to the road as you glimpse the idyllic beauty of Bridehead House, its lake and Little Bredy church. At the lane, turn left for the church. (From the path below the church you are allowed to walk in the grounds beside the lake.)

After visiting Little Bredy church retrace your steps along the lane for 100 metres. Take the left fork uphill for nearly half a mile. At the top turn right on a lane for 50 metres then left along Jubilee Trail. In 250 metres follow Jubilee Trail as it turns right. Ignore the path on the left, which goes towards Big Wood. Our Trail keeps its distance from Big Wood and becomes a wide way east with downland ahead. Keep the fence on your left and in half a mile you reach a tarmac road.

Cross the tarmac road and continue on Jubilee Trail which now veers south through Luscombe Plantation and passes a three storey house on the right. In half a mile just before the end of the woodland, turn sharp left on a grassy path which doubles back above the way you have just been. Go to the top of the hill, over a stile then head due east across the field to a line of beech trees. Here you are back on the first bridleway of this walk. Turn left and retrace your steps to Winterbourne Steepleton.

Dorchester's St Peter is on the busy high street. The statue of William Barnes, Dorset poet stands outside. (Walk 11)

Five Walks near Dorchester

Walk 11

Charminster – Puddletown – Stinsford – Dorchester

Walk in Thomas Hardy's footsteps across the wide rolling downs then through Puddletown Forest to visit his birthplace and the church where he left his heart. We also pass two stately homes in magnificent gardens and follow the River Frome to Dorchester.

Starting point: Charminster church; GR679927

Maps: Explorer 117 Landranger 194

Public transport: You will need to use local buses for this walk. Some do not run on Sunday. Bus and Train Timetables, Dorchester Area (2), published by Dorset County Council, is available from information offices. For guidance only, Monday to Saturday at the time of writing: 9.31 am bus 007 to Charminster from Trinity St C2 bus stop in Dorchester, (Coach House Travel Tel: 01305 267644); 9.35 and 11.35 am bus 184 from Dorchester Museum to Puddletown (Wilts and Dorset Tel: 01202 673555); 2.15 or 6.15 pm bus 184 from Puddletown to Dorchester.

Distance: 12 miles (or 6 miles, using buses)

Terrain: Downland followed by woodland. Gently undulating.

Notes

The Walk may be halved by using bus 184. A compass is recommended to follow the Explorer Map through Puddletown Forest.

The Churches

In Charminster, St Mary The Virgin is built of local stone with courses of flint, limestone and Ham Hill ashlar. 'Cerminster' in Saxon meant 'minster on the River Cerne'. Traces of 11th-century work can be seen in the nave, on either side of the chancel arch. This round-headed arch is 12th century with fine restored carving. The two arcades have the later 12th-century pointed arches. The south aisle was enlarged in 15th century to make a 'Wolfeton Chapel'. Wolfeton is a Tudor house built by Sir Thomas Trenchard to the south of Charminster. He is also thought to be responsible for the 16th-century pinnacled church tower. There is a devil's head in the south-east corner of the tower, 2 ½ metres from the ground. The 16th-century south porch has two gargoyles.

Puddletown's St Mary is mentioned in Domesday as Pitretone or Pirstone. It is really the 'tun' or town on the River Piddle. Victorians changed 'piddle' to 'puddle'. As you enter the church, which was built around 1400, 600 years drop away. The generous dimensions of the prosperous 15th century enfold you. The large church, including embattled tower, is almost entirely true Perpendicular. The panelled 15th-century oak roof was skilfully repaired in 1932. The Athelhampton Chantry contains six alabaster effigies from 13th to 15th centuries. The gallery of 1635 was probably later used as a minstrel gallery. Thomas Hardy's grandfather played the violincello here before 1800. Puddletown is 'Weatherbury' in 'Far From The Madding Crowd'.

St Michael's, Stinsford, is a pretty place, 13th century in character. A Saxon relief of a winged St Michael, much weathered from exposure above the west door, has been moved inside, in the south aisle. The square Norman font is of Purbeck marble. The short, square tower has an arch to the nave. The chancel arch is Early English. The Perpendicular south aisle with impressive gargoyles outside has an Early English arcade with fine carved capitals inside. Thomas Hardy made a sketch of these in his architectural notebook. Hardy was christened here and loved this church. His name for the hamlet is 'Mellstock' and it is the setting for 'Under The Greenwood Tree and the inspiration for his moving poem, 'Friends Beyond'. Hardy's ashes are in Poets Corner, Westminster Abbey but his heart is in Stinsford.

In Dorchester, St Peter's was built in the 15th century of grey Portland stone, trimmed with Ham Hill stone. It is Perpendicular in style with gargoyles on the tower and carved corbels where pillars hold the roof. The nave ceiling has fine 15th-century bosses. There is little to show of the original Norman church. Even the zigzag mouldings in the porch probably came from a priory and were fitted into the pointed arch. There is a plaque to John White in the porch. He is the rector who helped to rehouse parishioners after the 1613 AD town fire. Two poets are linked with the church. Thomas Hardy, when aged 16, helped in the restoration of 1856. William Barnes, the dialect poet was churchwarden here for a while. His statue stands outside the church on High West Street. He was also linked with Whitcombe and Winterborne Came churches – see Walk 34, Weymouth section.

The Walk

Go behind Charminster church to the stream, the River Cerne. Cross the footbridge and walk up the lane for 75 metres. Do not turn left but follow the curve of Mill Lane to the right. At a road junction turn left into Vicarage Gardens which becomes Vicarage Road. Walk through houses to the main

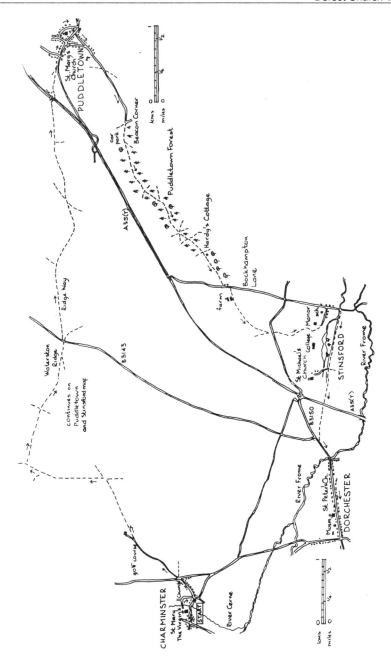

road. Cross to the track nearly opposite, ignore the path to the right and head for the golf course, served by a restaurant and bar open to the public. Just before this amenity, turn right into a footpath signposted 'Waterston Ridge'. The path is lined with hedges for half a mile. You emerge at a path junction and turn left at the signpost 'Piddlehinton Road'.

Go gently uphill with a hedge on the left. At the top of the field go through a gap on the left and continue with a hedge on the right. Ignore the path to the left. At the end of the hedge turn right on a track signposted 'Waterston Ridge'.

This track will take you east all the way to Puddletown. First the track dips into a new little plantation, then it rises to pass a green corrugated barn on your right. Higher still it crosses B3143 at Waterston Ridge, the highest point. Cross diagonally left with care. Ignore the bridleway on the right to Stinsford. Our track to Puddletown continues east and is known here as Ridge Way. It is sheltered by hedges on either side. Do not turn left or right. After one mile pass a bridleway to the left, a radio mast and a turning to Yellowham Wood on the right. The track bends left but go straight on through a gate. Cross the busy A35 on a new bridge, ignore the bridleway to the left and continue down the track passing playing fields on your right. You are on the edge of Puddletown now.

When you reach the junction with the old A35, turn left and cross to a bus shelter. *(Bear this in mind if you wish to shorten the walk and catch a bus to Dorchester)*. Continue along the pavement to traffic lights. Ignore A354 Blandford turning to the left and continue to the village store, passing a pub on the left. Cakes and other goodies can be had at the store. Cross to a bookshop and walk along Mill Street to the Square on the right. The church is at the other end of the Square.

From Puddletown church turn right away from the Square and follow the lane around the churchyard. Fork right for the High Street and cross to the road opposite, New Street. Follow New Street uphill, passing the gates of a school and continue along this quiet country lane for one mile to Beacon Corner and the entrance to Puddletown Forest.

Ignore the road up to the right (which leads to the car park) and go straight on into the forest heading west on a well defined bridleway. In 250 metres ignore the bridleway up to the left. Our way goes gently uphill and south-west. At the top at a wide cross track, go straight ahead. Continue for about 150 metres to crossways with views to the left through the trees to the hills beyond. Go straight on along the elevated path with conifers to the left and beech trees to the right. At a fork in your track, take the wider right-hand fork. This leads to a meeting of six ways. Avoid the main track to the right. The next track to the right has an off-shoot. It is the off-shoot we have to follow south-west downhill. In 150 metres avoid crosspaths with yellow arrows, well hidden in the conifers. A cottage can be seen ahead. Keep downhill for 200 metres to Hardy's Cottage and monument.

From Hardy's Cottage continue on the road past neighbouring cottages. Pass the car park and turning to Thorncombe to the left. At tarmac Bockhampton Lane turn left and walk past new cottages on your left and the entrance to a poultry farm on your right. Take the next turning right down a lane to a dead end by a barn. Go through the gate to the left of the barn and follow the path south-west across fields. The path is popular and well worn. Cross a tarmac road and into the grounds of Kingston Maurward College. This well-defined route crosses a driveway and passes between stables. To the right is Kingston Maurward House, built in 1720 for George Pitt. It has a large lake in front. To the left is the Old Manor House of 1591 in light grey stone. The bridleway curves left around the Manor House and away from the lake. Cross a cattle grid. Walled gardens are on the left. Follow the pathway out of the college grounds, passing bungalows on the left and the building department of the college on your right.

As you approach the village road, you pass the school on the left, attended for a while by Thomas Hardy and mentioned in 'Under The Greenwood Tree'. Turn right and go down the village road to the ancient bridge. Cross the river. Turn right along a tree-lined track which follows the river west. In half a mile turn right and cross over the river to visit nearby Stinsford church.

From Stinsford church return to the river track and resume your route west. Go under the A35 and through fields for another 350 metres to B3150, known here as London Road. Turn left and walk into Dorchester. The tall tower of Fordington church can be seen to the left. Cross the River Frome and you are in High East Street. Walk up to Saint Peter's Church and the County Museum housed in a building that was once All Saints Church, both on the right. Trinity Street is the next turning left. Go down here for Tourist Information Office and buses to Charminster.

Walk 12

Milborne St Andrew – Tolpuddle – Affpuddle – Turners Puddle

This walk is packed with interest: there is the museum at Tolpuddle to commemorate the first union of workmen in this country, The Tolpuddle Martyrs. Later we climb the Iron Age fort of Weatherby Castle with a hidden obelisk. There are also some beautiful churches near the River Piddle. In summer there are comfrey and forget-me-nots. In winter, snowdrops and possible flooding:

> *Hey diddle, Hey Diddle, Hey diddle,*
> *I live on the banks of the Piddle*
> *But if it should flood,*
> *There is no doubt I should*
> *Be in Piddle right up to my middle.*

Starting point: Milborne St Andrew Church; GR802974

Maps: Explorer 117 Landranger 194

Distance: 8½ miles or can be shortened to 7½ miles

Terrain: gently undulating

The Churches

In Milborne, the flint church of St Andrew has a fine Norman doorway with small columns, scallop capitals and zigzag moulding. The nave wagon roof and the tower are Perpendicular. The church was enlarged in 1876 and the chancel was rebuilt. The pointed transitional Norman chancel arch was re-set in the wall of the vestry. There is a plain Norman font.

St John's, in Tolpuddle also has some of its Norman past: the north and south doorways. The north doorway, now blocked was known as the 'sin' door; at christenings evil spirits were expected to leave by that door. The present building of flint and ashlar is mainly 13th century. The beam roof is 14th century. The arches of the north transept and those of the north arcade are Decorated. The lower part of the tower is 13th century flint and ashlar. The upper 15th-century part is rubble. Of the Tolpuddle Martyrs only James Hammett returned to the village and his much visited grave is in the churchyard.

Affpuddle, St Laurence is a delightful church on a bank of the River Puddle. The Perpendicular pinnacled tower is chequered ashlar and flint. The trefoil arch of the south door dates from about 1230. The chancel arch is Early English and there are early Decorated windows. In 1547.Thomas

Lyllington, a monk from Cerne Abbas, became vicar here after the Dissolution of the Monasteries. Was he responsible for the carvings on the pulpit of monks who are half fool?

Turnerspuddle's Holy Trinity is a tiny early 16th-century church of flint and stone. Although redundant as a church and privately owned, it is still cared for in this quiet corner. The owner is Mrs Debenham of Debenhams and Freebody.

The Walk

St Andrew's is at the upper end of Chapel Lane in Milborne. Go down the lane to a footpath on the right which takes you south through remnants of parkland. One stately pillar still stands in the middle of the field. Go past this and continue across meadows with the stream on your left. In over half a mile you come to an arc of beech trees. Cross to the next field and keep straight on to pick up the farm track which comes from the left and heads south-west uphill to a small copse. Enter by the rickety gate and go through the copse. Come out at an elevated field and continue south-west on a wide track for about one mile. You can see the traffic on the new bypass ahead. Come down through a muddy farmyard between barns and head for the bypass. Cross over and Tolpuddle is 300 metres ahead. You come out at the main street with Martyrs' Inn on your left.

Turn right for the church and further along on the right you will find TUC Memorial Cottages Museum. Retrace your steps along the main street passing Martyrs' Inn on your left. You can now walk peacefully through the village where cars and lorries used to roar. At the eastern edge of the village, past the Methodist Chapel, turn right over a stile. Continue down a field with a hedge on your right and turn left at the bottom. Head south-east over water meadows for over half a mile. Just after the barn on the left, make for the stream with willows on the right. A slightly raised grassy path takes you to a stile onto a tarmac road. Turn right and walk along the road, cross over a stream and Affpuddle church is on the right.

From Affpuddle, retrace your steps over the bridge and along the road passing two footpaths on the left, one of which brought you here. Just past the converted barn on the left look for a footpath sign in the hedge on the right-hand side of the road. Turn right to resume your south-east course down a path with a hedge on your right. In half a mile veer right and cross to a stream. Continue on route with the hedge on your left now. In 75 metres cross a private drive to a footpath opposite. This leads to another country road. Cross with care to the enclosed track opposite.

Continue south-east and in 200 metres Jubilee Trail joins from Briantspuddle on the right. You are now on Jubilee Trail heading east. In 300 metres you pass a bridleway on the left signposted to Kite Hill. You will

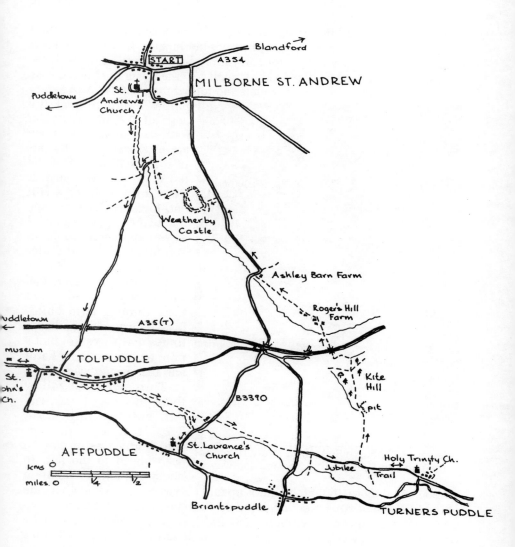

need this later *(or you could shorten the walk by one mile, miss out Turners Puddle and turn left now)*. To continue the full walk, ignore the path on the left and Turners Puddle is less than half a mile away. You can see the church from your track.

From Turners Puddle retrace your steps to the bridleway to Kite Hill. (I have seen buzzards wheeling over the trees but no kites here). Head north uphill to enter woods with a quarry on your right. Continue up the well defined path, do not be beguiled by other paths. At the top of the hill a grassy path leads straight on but we turn left and follow the main track to an apparent T-junction at the edge of the wood. If you look carefully, in fact we are at crossways. The tarmac track downhill to the left is the one we need. It leads away from Kite Hill and towards the A35. The roar of the bypass increases as you approach. Go down and follow the road under the bypass to reach Rogers Hill Farm on the other side. There is a well-defined track through farm buildings. It curves left and continues north-west for half a mile to Ashley Barn Farm and the tarmac road.

Turn right and follow the road which then veers left, heading north-west. The Iron age mound, Weatherby Castle can be seen ahead to the left. In about one mile turn left on

View from Milborne St Andrew church. Behind the photographer is a fine Norman doorway.

a well signed footpath which climbs up and curves round to the other side of the hill. When you enter woodland on this side, you find the lone, hidden obelisk with the inscription '1761 EMP – Edmund Morton Pleydell'. Come out of the woodland and continue until you reach a hedge. Follow the hedge down to the stream below. Cross here and keep straight on to the same arc of trees you passed before. Turn right and retrace your steps to Milborne St Andrew.

Walk 13

Tincleton – Moreton

This walk passes through meadowland, sandy common land and much woodland. Near the River Frome at Moreton, a unique church has risen from the ashes.

Starting point: Tincleton church at a T-junction of minor roads. GR776918

Maps: Outdoor Leisure 15 and Landranger 194

Distance: 8½ miles, can be shortened to 6½ miles

Terrain: one slope up and one down, repeated on return

The Churches

Tincleton's St John the Evangelist stands near the old school. Both are the work of Benjamin Ferrey. This 19th-century church is in Early English style with a Norman font. Tincleton was valued at 20 shillings in Domesday.

In Moreton, there is the grey stone church of St Nicholas, built in 1777 by James Frampton and replacing an earlier building. It is Georgian Gothic

Moreton church has clear glass windows that were engraved by
Laurence Whistler in 1958

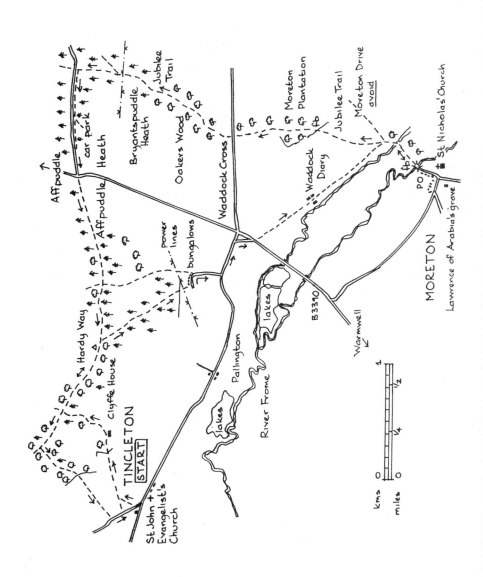

in style and retains its wide 18th-century nave. In 1940 a bomb damaged the church. It has been beautifully restored with a new apsidal east end. There are 12 engraved windows by Lawrence Whistler (1958). These alone are enough to draw admirers to this light, spacious church. Others come to visit the grave of Lawrence of Arabia in the cemetery across the road.

The Walk

Take the road opposite Tincleton church and in 50 metres turn right on a path rising gently up towards Clyffe House. You are heading north-east and keep this large Tudor style house with tall chimneys in view. At a corner of a wood you enter the grounds through a little gate and a narrow path. Turn left along the driveway around to the back of the house, built in 1842. When you reach the walled garden, go no further. The footpath is hidden in the shrubbery on the left. It is a narrow way through evergreen bushes. Other footprints confirm that you are on the path. It becomes a wider track through trees for 300 metres. Do not be tempted onto paths to the right until you reach a big gate. Go through beside the gate and in another 50 metres you come to wide crosstracks.

Turn right through more woodland heading south-east for half a mile. You emerge to open heathland with a wide track coming from the right and a small pond down on the right. Do not turn right but keep on course along a track across gorse-covered hillside with distant views to the right. Ignore a track to the left. Just after this, a trig point is hidden in undergrowth on the left. Next you come to a line of posts marked 'M'. Turn right here and go down a narrow footpath to find a bridleway sign on a post. Follow the bridleway signs, go across a wide track and head south-east down through woodland for nearly one mile. Do not be tempted to divert down any side paths.

Go under overhead cables at a bungalow. Turn left then right and follow the service road past more bungalows and down to the road.

This is the road back to Tincleton. Those wishing to shorten the walk can come back here after visiting Moreton church.

To continue to Moreton, turn left and walk along the road passing on the right a village notice board and a track down to watercress beds. In 250 metres turn right and the busy B3390 is 100 metres ahead. Our footpath is diagonally to the right opposite. You are heading south-east on a wide farm track. Go through farm buildings known as Waddock Dairy. Continue on route for another half a mile, passing to the left the footpath which you will need for the return walk. The narrow river is on your right. Enter woodland, turn right, cross the narrow river then the wide, main stream of the River Frome on a footbridge. You are in Moreton. Walk up past the post office and stores on your right. The church is 50 metres ahead on the left.

From Moreton church return to the footbridge over the main River Frome and follow the Jubilee Trail signs. These lead to the stile where you entered the wood.

For the short cut keep straight on and retrace your steps with the narrow river on your left.

For the full walk bear right and cross the field heading north along Jubilee Trail which passes the corner of a wood. Keep on course through the next field with several stiles and enter woodland, Moreton Plantation, over a footbridge. The footpath through the plantation is quite well-marked with Jubilee Trail signs, but there are bends. At the first T-junction turn right. At a fork in the path, bear left. At a second T-junction, where you can see a rusty old tank ahead, turn left then right along the side of the wood.

Cross the tarmac road and enter more woodland, Oakers Wood on an enclosed Jubilee Trail. In one mile at Bryantspuddle Heath there has been forest clearance. Go under overhead cables, pass a mere down on the right and you reach crosspaths. Turn left at a wide track and then right up a steep path to emerge at the edge of the wood. Here you leave Jubilee Trail.

Do not go onto the road, but turn left and walk down the grassy track between the edge of the wood and the road until you reach a parking area with picnic tables. Beyond this point the road meets the B3390. At this T-junction continue across the B-road and enter the woods. Follow the wide forestry track for one and a half miles, passing the familiar 'M' posts on your left and retracing your steps past the pond and through the wood.

After 200 metres you reach the intersection where you joined this track originally and can see the gate down the path to your left. Keep straight ahead north-west until you reach the first turning to the left. Avoid the bridleway with a sign ahead of you. Turn left down a sunken lane and ignore paths to right and left. At the bottom go through the gate in front, through farm buildings and down to the road. Turn left and you can see Tincleton church ahead.

Walk 14

Hilton – Milton Abbey – St Catherine's Chapel (and, optionally, to Bingham's Melcombe)

This is a varied walk from wild downland near Bulbarrow to park and meadowland with some woods. The churches also range from the conventional village to the magnificent abbey, the ancient humble refuge to the prized estate church.

Starting point: Hilton church; GR783030

Maps: Explorer 117 and Landranger 194

Distance: 8 miles or 10 miles

Terrain: Some hills, some flat land

The Churches

Hilton's All Saints has come a long way from its probable Saxon origins. Stones on either side of the chancel arch may be Saxon. The present Perpendicular church contains some grand treasures. The beautiful windows of the north aisle were brought from Milton Abbey after the Dissolution. The fan vaulted south porch was probably also an acquisition from the abbey; it seems to have been inserted after the church was built. The medieval panels, paintings of the Apostles on the tower walls are part of a large screen from Milton Abbey. They were given to the church in 1774. The village of Hilton still has some pretty thatched cottages and, sited below Bulbarrow, makes a fine picture.

Milton Abbey is a glorious church in golden Ham Hill stone. It stands in a wide valley served by a little stream with wooded hills all around. The first building here was a collegiate college founded by King Athelston in 933. In 964 King Edwin replaced the secular priests with Benedictine monks. They thrived and a market town grew up around the abbey. In 1309. the Norman church burnt down and the monks started work on an ambitious new building. Abbot William Middleton (1461-1525) supervised. The 15th-century tower stands above the Crossing. The early 16th-century north transept contains the famous Damer monument (1775) by A. Carlini. It depicts a man mourning his wife and stands alone in front of the huge Damer and Sackville window. The windows are Perpendicular in the north transept and late Decorated in the south transept. The south window is a magnificent 'Tree of Jesse' (1847) by Augustus Pugin. In the two western bays the lower walls are faced with flint. There is a fine organ in the north aisle. The chancel has seven bays. There is no nave. In 1539 at the Dissolution of the Monasteries, the monks left Milton Abbey. Inside this light, spacious church are beautiful monuments. The details of these are in the illustrated guide. *See Walk 3, Milton Abbas for more on Joseph Damer.*

St Catherine's Chapel, perhaps started by King Athelstan, is a humble naighbour in the woods near Milton Abbey. The chapel of rough flint, Ham Hill and local limestone is Norman. Medieval maids came here to pray for husbands. The true purpose of this chapel can be read on the door jamb with its small columns and leaf capitals. The inscription promises 120 days' indulgence to wayfarers.

Bingham's Melcombe church of St Andrew stands close to the lovely irregular manor house which we can only glimpse. Most of the 14th-century church is flint. The tower is stone. The south-east part of the 19th-century chancel is a blend of flint, brown ironstone, Purbeck marble and Ham Hill stone. There is a Bingham Chapel. The Binghams were lords of the manor. There is also a late fifteenth century Horsey Chapel. The Horsey family held nearby Higher Melcombe in sixteenth century. A walk on these estates is a ghostly trail over a secluded bit of England past.

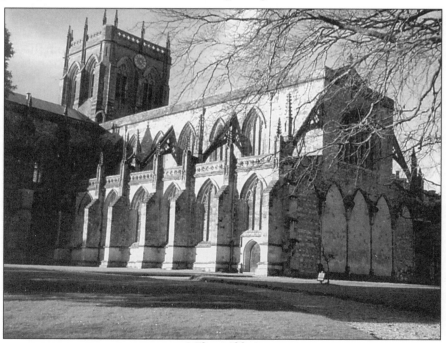

Milton Abbey

The Walk

From Hilton church cross the road to Knapp Lane opposite and walk between cottages about 75 metres. The lane curves left, we keep straight on up a track known locally as Brick Lane. This climbs up above the village in a hedge-lined way. Towards the top, avoid paths to the left and a crater on the right. The track emerges through a gate at Greenhill Down Nature Reserve.

Turn right here and head south passing a small pond on the right. There are fine views over Delcombe to the left. In about 150 metres you descend through woodland for over half a mile to come out at the breath taking beauty of the amphitheatre of wooded slopes around Milton Abbey.

Turn left and follow the tarmac lane as it curves in front of Milton Abbey School. Pass the school entrance on the right and seek the lane on the left up to St Catherine's Chapel. If the school is open to visitors, you can visit it and the Abbey.

Otherwise, follow the access track below the chapel. The farmer has kindly agreed to let me describe this track as a 'Permissive path' (see the sketch map). The path is open at the farmer's discretion. It leads south and east up to a small housing estate where you turn right on a footpath down to Milton Abbas. Walk down through the village to crossroads at the bottom. The left turn is marked to Milborne St Andrew. We turn right along the road to a lodge then left along a lakeside footpath to the Abbey and back.

After visiting the Abbey, follow the main road marked to Milborne St Andrew. In 200 metres the main road bends left but we keep straight on up the steep slope of a minor road, advertised as leading to a Rare Breeds Centre. Follow the road as it curves right through woodland then left out of the wood. In 250 metres, turn right into a firm track towards woodland. At a Y-junction take the right fork which takes you in the same north-west direction with woodland on the right. The wood recedes and the path curves gently to the left passing a house on the right. Continue on the path heading north-west to a tarmac road.

(Turn right on the tarmac road. Walk for about half a mile along the road and turn right at the first footpath for a short cut to Hilton. See map and later notes.)

For the full walk cross the tarmac road to the footpaths opposite. There are two fingerposts. Take the one ahead to Bingham's Melcombe. It follows the line of the hedge on the left and leads down to a wooded corner. Go down through wooded slopes curving left then right to find the remote hamlet below.

Turn right when you reach the tarmac lane. In about 50 metres on the left, slip through a gate and follow the left-hand hedge alongside Devil's Brook until you reach a footbridge with a lake to your right. Go over the footbridge to the church and the nearby private manor house. You may

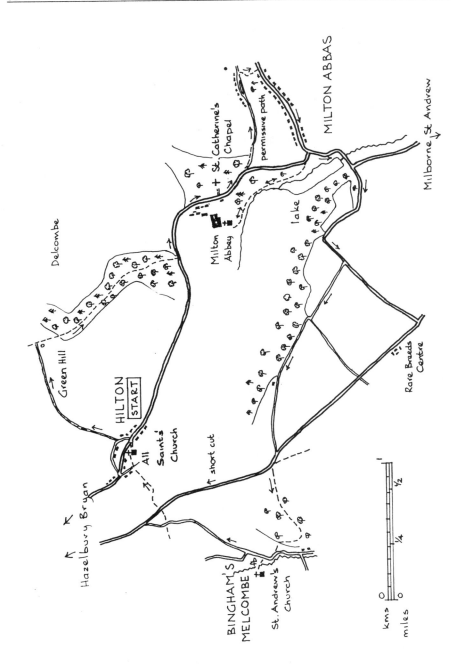

have time to wander around Bingham's Melcombe on public footpaths as shown on the O.S. map.

To return to Hilton from Bingham's Melcombe, retrace your steps over the footbridge and the path to the tarmac lane. Slip back through the gate, turn left and walk along the lane until it bends to the left. You take the enclosed track on the right up Combe Hill. At crosspaths turn right and walk up to the tarmac road.

Cross the road to the footpath opposite. The short cut joins here. Go straight across the field, find a woodland path and descend steeply. When you emerge from the wood, you can see the church and village of Hilton 150 metres ahead.

St Catherine's chapel is an ancient refuge in woods near Milton Abbey

Walk 15

Cerne Abbas – Nether Cerne – Godmanstone (and also to Sydling St Nicholas)

This walk in the heart of Dorset takes in four villages (three if you miss out Sydling) and their much-loved ancient churches. Each has a charm of its own. In Cerne Abbas we have the bonus of visiting the site of the Benedictine abbey. We pass a variety of interesting old cottages and Georgian houses. Above the car park to the north-west is Giant Hill with its much-photographed 180ft outline of a naked man cut in the turf, the god of fertility or a sheep-eating giant slain by the people of Cerne Abbas?

Starting point: Picnic area and car park, Kettle Bridge on the north side of Cerne Abbas; GR664016

Maps: Explorer 117 and Landranger 194

Distance: 8 miles or 11 miles (or, with the bus, 5½ miles)

Public transport: Bus 216 (First Southern National Tel: 01305 783645) will take you back to Cerne Abbas from Godmanstone. At the time of writing it leaves Smiths Arms at 11.17 am, 12.17 and 1.47 pm also 3.47 and 4.37 pm Monday to Saturday.

Terrain: Varied. Some riverside, some hill and some ridge walking.

The Churches

In Cerne Abbas, St Mary's has bands of golden stone and flint, as do other buildings in this delightful little town. The church stands near the site of the Benedictine Abbey, built in 987. Monks built St Mary's Church in 1300. The Early English windows in the chancel are original and the 15th-century east window may have come from the Abbey which was dissolved in 1539. 14th-century wall paintings near the altar show John The Baptist and the Annunciation. The fine church tower with gargoyles is late 15th century. The early 16th-century Madonna and Child carving above the west door of the tower is lucky to have escaped destruction under Cromwell. Also of interest are 15th-century stone rood screen and Jacobean pulpit.

Nether Cerne's All Saints has bands of local rubble stone and flint with freestone dressings. The nearby 17th-century manor also has bands of flint and stone. They stand together in a quiet spot beside the River Cerne. The church is in the care of the Churches Conservation Trust. It was originally a chapelry to Cerne Abbey. The present building: nave, chancel and south chapel is 13th century with windows of that period. The Perpendicular tower is unusual in having angels as gargoyles. Also unusual is the Norman font of Purbeck stone.

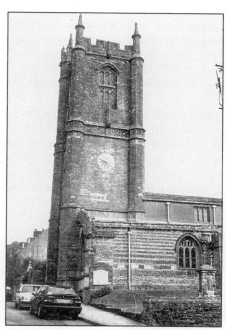

Cerne Abbas is a graceful 14th-century church in this ancient little town

Godmanstone's Holy Trinity, built of stone and flint, is also in the valley of the Cerne. The 15th-century church has a low pinnacled Perpendicular tower. The chancel arch is Norman. The south doorway has zigzag moulding and a tympanum in Norman style. In the chancel is a Victorian monument to two 19-year-old girls who died from catching a cold by sitting on the downs – a warning to us!

In Sydling, the village and church of St Nicholas are built of bands of flint and stone. They stand in the valley of Sydling Water, a pure clear stream running into the River Frome at Grimstone. The church is on a gentle rise south-west in the village. The exterior is full of character with gruesome gargoyles, some acting as water spouts, and elegant buttresses propping up the south aisle. The bishop's mitre above the porch may belong to Nicholas Longspee, Bishop of Salisbury in the 14th century. The church is mainly 15th century; the Perpendicular tower is the oldest part. The 18th-century chancel holds many memorials. A stone corbel in the shape of a man's head is in the squint near the chancel. The very old font is believed to have been cut from a Roman capital.

The Walk

From Kettle Bridge car park go to the entrance, turn left and walk about 25 metres to the River Cerne. Turn right and walk beside the river into Cerne Abbas. The river curves to the right and you cross it, turning left into Abbey Street near the Town Pond. The Abbey's Guest House and the Abbot's Porch are at one end of Abbey Street and the church at the other.

From Cerne Abbas church, head for the main street, Long Street and turn right. Go past Duck Street on the right and New Inn on the left. Turn left into Back Lane then immediately right onto a footpath leading to a bridge over the river. Once across, turn left on a footpath which follows the river. On your right is the large Tithe Barn dating from 1350. This was the storehouse of tithes, paid by the villagers to the Abbey.

Now you have a choice of paths; a permissive path follows the course of the river and heads south over fields to a farm track near some buildings. *The public footpath heads south-east to a corner of the field, through trees and another field to reach the same farm track.* Whichever route you take, turn left onto the farm track and go along it, across the river and up a hill, Black Hill.

Part way up the hill there is a thick hedgerow skirting it. Turn right here and go through or just above the hedge. Follow the hedge and in less than half a mile the path goes down to a stile on the right. Go through to a wide expanse of sloping fields with the river on the right. Head south to a farm gate and continue south on a farm track. Pound Farm can be seen ahead.

Go straight on through the farmyard towards a field slope with a wood at the top. Keep to the right-hand edge of the field, avoiding the wood. The stile is hidden in the right-hand corner of the field. Go through to the next field with private lakes ahead. The path veers to the left towards woodland. Walk through the wood on an enclosed path to Nether Cerne. Cross the secluded road to the tracks opposite. Avoid the forked track to the left and take the lower track. Nether Cerne church and House are down to the right.

After visiting Nether Cerne church, return to resume your southerly course on the chosen track which soon takes you along the river bank. Godmanstone is half a mile away. Avoid two footbridges over the river and take the third bridge, signposted to Godmanstone. 'The smallest pub in England', possibly closed at present, is on the right and the church is across the main road A352 opposite.

From Godmanstone church return to the A352, turn right and up a nearby bridleway on the right through Manor Farm with organic milk and cream for sale. The bridleway track climbs up for over half a mile heading north-west to downland. At the top inside a copse on the right someone has made rock carvings. Our route is to the left of the copse, go through the gate with many bridleway signs and admire the wide views over the wild valley and across to Break Heart Hill on the Roman Road.

For the shorter way back to Cerne Abbas: After going through the gate with many bridleway signs, turn right and follow the bridleway north along the ridge with views down to the left. Do not turn left or right. At a nearby open space make for the corner of a hedge ahead. Go through the gate to the next field and continue north with the hedge on your left. In about 300 metres cross to the other side of the hedge and keep on route, north-west for over one mile with the hedge on your right. Look for the buildings of Higher City Farm ahead. Just past the farm, the longer route on the Wessex Ridgeway joins the track as we continue north to a tarmac road.

Both Routes

The tall aerial on Buckland Hill can be seen ahead. Cross the road with care and head for the aerial walking on a firm track. There are more fine views down to the left. In over half a mile go past the aerial and turn right, leaving the Wessex Ridgeway. Cross a field and walk down to enter a wood near the centre of its boundary. Inside the wood, avoid the track to the left and follow the path downhill.

Come out of the woodland to enjoy the view over the vale to Cerne Abbas. Follow the slope of the hill to the left and south-east into the vale between woods. Head for a carriage hut, which you pass on your right. Follow the wide track which curves round another hill on the left. In about 200 metres you reach a junction of tracks. We want the path to the right follow-

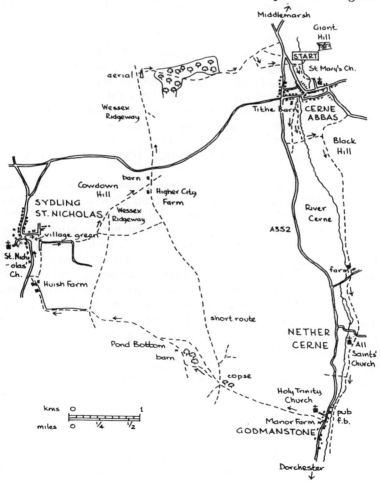

ing the hedge down nearly to the bottom of the slope. Turn left and at a gap in the hedge, cross the fence into the next field. Head for the white house on the other side. Steps here take you down to the main road. You can cross the field opposite or make a slight detour left along the road then sharp right back to the car park at Kettle Bridge.

To return on the longer route to Cerne Abbas via Sydling St Nicholas: at the top of the hill, after Godmanstone, keep the trees with the carved stones on your right and go through the gate with all the bridleway signs. Turn right and walk to the nearby field boundary. Turn left keeping the flimsy fence on your right. Go down into a narrow track through gorse and scrub. Over to the hill on your left, you can see two hedge rings and shrubs below – a face on the landscape?

In 300 metres turn right along lonely Pond Bottom. No pond can be seen but you pass Reynards Copse on the right and buzzards may be wheeling overhead. Pass a rusty barn on your left and follow the farm track north-west. In about half a mile at a fence corner, the track bends left and climbs gradually to cross bridleways. Carry straight on. The track becomes a concrete farm road. Follow it downhill for another half a mile as it curves right and passes cottages, barns and the old farmhouse of Huish Farm. At a T-junction with sawmills on the right, turn left to the tarmac lane. Turn right and walk along the lane into Sydling St Nicholas. At cross lanes turn up left to the church.

From Sydling St Nicholas Church return to the village and cross to a stream and East Street which leads to the Green. Cross the Green diagonally towards a seat and take the concrete track between houses in the corner. The Wessex Ridgeway is the first turning to the left, heading east and up-hill. Follow this track with tall hedges on either side for about 250 metres. As soon as the track veers right, we go straight on through a gate and along a shelf above a shallow valley with a slight ridge on our right. The lightly marked track continues in the next field up to a gate where bridleways fork. Go straight on, that is the right-hand fork and follow the hedge on your left up to the main ridge track at the top. Turn left and walk along the ridge in a north-easterly direction. Pass trees at crosspaths then a ring of trees near the top of Cowdown Hill.

Higher City Farm can be seen ahead. Go past the big barn then turn left to join the shorter route to Cerne Abbas. See above.

Pentridge church stands in a remote hamlet below
hills where prehistoric monuments abound. (Walk 20)

Five Walks near Shaftesbury

Walk 16

Saint James's Village – Shaftesbury

From the village at the foot of Shaftesbury Hill, you climb up to the site of the ancient abbey and enjoy the extensive views. Explore this town contained on the hill and saunter back to St James below. The Parish Church of St Peter, Shaftesbury is usually open between 10 am and 4 pm, March to November, when volunteers welcome visitors.

Starting point: near the Church of St James – as you approach Shaftesbury from the south-west on the B3091 from Manston, you come to this prominent church in the lee of Shaftesbury's slopes; GR858224

Maps: Explorer 118 and Landranger 183

Distance: 2 miles

Terrain: one steep slope up and one down

The Churches

Under the brow of Shaftesbury, the little village of stone houses has its own church of St James. The original building stood on open ground until about 1724 when the stone wall was built. The old church decayed with the poverty of its parishioners. The Victorians resited it (1866-7) 100 feet west of the original position and built a church in Decorated and Perpendicular styles. The chancel windows of the old church were used as windows for the aisles. It is a large church with a tall tower, a clear landmark for those arriving from the south or for those looking down from Shaftesbury above.

In Shaftesbury, King Alfred founded the Benedictine Abbey in 888. His daughter, Aethelgive, was the first abbess. The abbey grew and prospered. The bones of the martyred King Edward brought pilgrims. The power and wealth of the abbey drew the attention of Henry VIII who had it destroyed at the Dissolution in 1539. Now we can trace the floor of this once great building in the Abbey Garden, next to Park Walk.

Also in Shaftesbury, St Peter's has its front entrance next to the town hall and its tower on the edge of the steep slope of Gold Hill. The church is mainly Perpendicular with fine vaulting in the west porch. In the past the vault was used as a cellar for the pub next door. 'The spirit above is the Spirit Divine, the spirit below is the spirit of wine' is a local saying. The crypt is now a delightful chapel.

The Walk

From the church, walk up Saint James Street through the pretty stone cottages. At the junction, turn left up the famous Gold Hill. The huge buttresses on the left were 14th- and 15th-century supports for the Abbey walls. They have survived the Abbey. Turn round to admire the view. At the top of Gold Hill you come to the Museum, the Town Hall and the Church of St Peter.

From St Peter's walk past the Town Hall to a corner between shops where there is a signpost to Park Walk and the Abbey. Park Walk is short but spectacular. Delightful views to Win Green Hill, Melbury Hill, the Blackmore Vale and Bulbarrow beyond draw you to the parapet. Do not forget to visit the Abbey remains on the right. The market cross, moved from

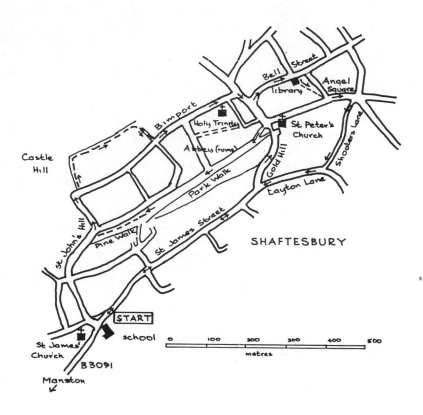

Cobbled Gold Hill has been much filmed and photographed

Angel Square, stands on the site of the altar. Holy Trinity, with its tall tower, stands near the Abbey and is now a centre for advice and care.

Continue along Park Walk and bear slightly right into Pine Walk, through trees to St John's Hill. Beware of traffic here. Go uphill for 50 metres and the footpath to Castle Hill is just around the right-hand bend. Here you have views north to Wiltshire and on a clear day to the Mendips.

Keep along the edge of Castle Hill to Bimport and turn left. At the end turn right and then left along Bell Street to the modern library. Here you turn immediately right and cut down through a car park to Angel Square. At the south of the square there is a walk down Shooters Lane to Layton Lane at the bottom. Turn right along Layton Lane, pass Gold Hill on your right and retrace your steps down through St James to the church.

Walk 17

West Stour – Stour Provost – Fifehead Magdalen

This is a walk which takes in three golden villages near the River Stour.

Starting point: Village Hall, Church Street, West Stour; GR784228
Maps: Explorer 129 and Landranger 183
Distance: 4½ miles
Terrain: gently undulating. May be muddy in places

The Churches

St Mary's is tucked into a slope off a residential road in West Stour. The church is built of squared and coursed rubble with ashlar dressings and has a stone slate roof. Although the nave and tower were rebuilt in 1840, the Victorians kept the original shape. The chancel has 13th-century lancet windows One to the south has a 16th-century trefoil head. The west gallery is Perpendicular. From 1818 to 1859 an orchestra played in the gallery. The absent minded priest of West Stour is thought to be the inspiration for Parson Adams in Henry Fielding's 'Tom Jones'. Fielding had a house at nearby East Stour.

Stour Provost is a quiet place of mellow yellow cottages and old farmhouses. In their midst the 14th-century church St Michael's stands benign. Perhaps the 15th-century gargoyles at the top of the embattled tower have driven off all evil spirits! Inside, the chancel arch is medieval. The 16th-century chancel roof is low pitched and has fine carvings, similar to those of Marnhull. Much of the church was restored by the Victorians. Even before the 19th century, the poor of the parish were catered for and a generous diet of beer, bread, cheese and vegetables supplied. The church

Stour Provost has an ancient, peaceful church above the River Stour

may originally have been dedicated to St Leger. The nunnery of St Leger in De Preaux, Normandy held the church in 11th century. Henry V took it away from France. Edward IV gave it to King's College, Cambridge. A new church was built in 1302 when the Bishop of Salisbury demanded that it be properly consecrated.

St Mary Magdalene is at the east end of the small village of Fifehead Magdalen. 'As pleasant a spot as any in the county', according to John Hutchins in 18th century. From its elevated position, we should be able to look across the River Stour to Stour Provost but trees bar the view. The church is 14th century. There are records that an earlier church here was given to the Abbey of St Augustine, Bristol in 12th century. The north chapel was added in 18th century. The church was restored 1904-5. There are many monuments to the Newman family.

The Walk

From the village hall go north up the road to the nearby church. Then retrace your steps back down the road, passing the village hall and continuing south to the A30. Turn right to a large wayside inn, the Ship Inn and cross the main road to a footpath opposite. This heads south-east over two pastures. In 300 metres you cross a footbridge over the River Stour. Veer left and follow the river for 200 metres. The river takes a sharp turn to the north but we maintain a south-west course to farm gates ahead. Cross a stream and head diagonally right up to a corner of the field. Stour Provost can be seen up on the right. Turn right when you reach a firm track which takes you south into the village, passing idyllic riverside cottages. In 300 metres you reach Stour Provost church by a side path on the left, Church Lane.

From Stour Provost church return along the same path and cross the road diagonally right to a lane between cottages. At the end of the tarmac, this lane curves left to a gate and stile and then down a field through trees towards the river. Pass below a magnificent old building, once a mill beside the River Stour. Turn sharp right to cross two footbridges then turn left with the river on your left. You are heading west and Fifehead Magdalen can be seen half a mile ahead on an elevation. When you reach the second hedgerow on your right, cross two stiles and turn right away from the river. Follow the hedge, as it grows taller and thicker, uphill. Turn right at the tarmac road and Fifehead Magdalen church is ahead. Make a note of the footpath which you pass on your right.

From Fifehead Magdalen church return to the nearby footpath you passed before. Turn left and you are on the edge of what were the grounds of the manor house. Stour Provost can be seen below. At the corner of the field, turn left away from this view and head north. Ignore an opening into a field to the left and follow the hedgerow to a stile and gate. Cross the first field diagonally left to a stile. Continue on the same line across the corner of the second field. Enter the third field and bear right. You are on a northerly course with the hedgerow on your right. The busy A30 and a few houses of West Stour are half a mile ahead. Go down to a footbridge in a hedgerow and cross the next field to a stile. A narrow path leads up to A30. Turn right and you have to walk along this busy road for 100 metres before you come to a pavement, which takes you to the Ship Inn and Church Street.

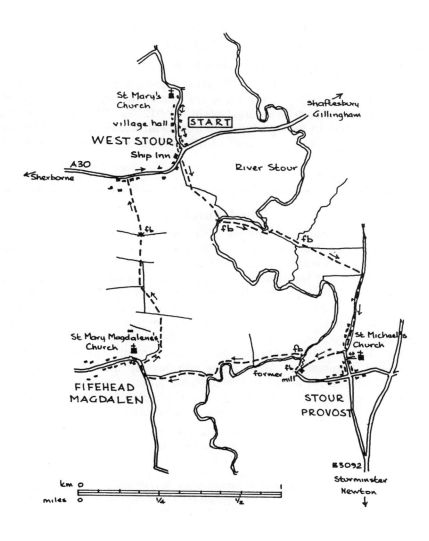

Walk 18

Fontmell Magna – Sutton Waldron – Iwerne Minster – Ashmore Forest

The three very different churches of this walk are in villages beside the A350 Blandford Forum to Shaftesbury Road.

Starting point: Fontmell Magna, the picnic site, Mill Strreet; GR870168.

Maps: Explorer 118 and Landranger 183, 184

Distance: 8 miles or 4 miles with a bus back

Public transport: Buses 182 and 183 serve these villages. They run at intervals of over 1 hour until 5. 53 pm There is a lunch time gap in the service between 1.09 and 3.46 pm (Wilts and Dorset Tel: 01202 673555). It is possible to shorten the walk by taking a bus back from Iwerne to Fontmell. You would then miss out on the scenic part of the walk over downs and through Ashmore Forest.

Terrain: hilly in parts

The Churches

St Andrew's in Fontmell Magna is a Perpendicular church built of greensand ashlar. The lower part of the tower is 15th century. The main body of the church was rebuilt in 1863 and a third stage added to the tower. The church is most impressive with a parapet of quatrefoils. The Dorset historian, Rev. John Hutchins thought this church one of the handsomest in the diocese. The font, carved in greensand stone, is Norman. 'Funtmell' is mentioned in the oldest West Saxon Charter of 704 when land was granted to Coinred, father of King Ina. From the Norman Conquest until the Dissolution Fontmell came under the domain of the most powerful convent in England, Shaftesbury Abbey. The affluence of the village was augmented by the clear flowing Fontmell Brook which drove three mills and supplied a brewery and a foundry. Fontmell Magna is loved by visitors and villagers. William Lush, a local man expressed his love in poetry:

> *'I shall turn again to Fontmell*
> *In the Autumn of my days,*
> *And I'll walk among the hollows*
> *And narrow winding ways,*
> *Which from Fontmell Wood to Compton,*
> *And from Twyford back to Pen,*
> *Are within the sound of Fontmell*
> *Bells and dear to Fontmell Men'.*

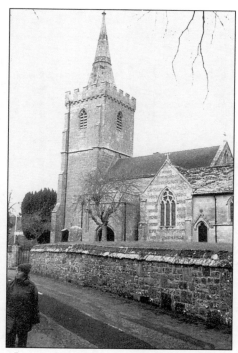

Iwerne Minster is an important ancient church with a medieval stone spire

The church of St Bartholomew was built in Sutton Waldron in 1874 of flint with a rendered tower and soaring spire, this church is described by John Betjeman as 'one of the best and most lovely examples of Victorian architecture'. Canon Huxtable, rector from 1834, arranged and paid for the new church, close to the discarded Saxon ruin. The Gothic structure must have been like a Phoenix rising from ashes. A Bronze Age barrow used to stand just north of Sutton Clump, indicating a settlement here 3000 years ago. 1086 Domesday Survey mentions 25 males, quite a sizeable village then. Farming has always been the main livelihood. The Common Field System has operated from Saxon times to the early 19th century. This meant that each farmer had a share of the fertile strips near the village and the chalk strips in the downs. The narrow ledges can be clearly seen. At the end of 18th century, men were drawn from the land into cod fishing in boats leaving Poole for Newfoundland. Another source of income, especially for women and children was button making. This ended in 1851 when machines took over.

Saint Mary's, Iwerne Minster. The Saxons established an Augustinian Mynstre here and brought Christianity to the surrounding villages. In 888 King Alfred founded Shaftesbury Abbey and in 956 King Eadwig gave Iwerne and the five churches of the Minster to the abbess. The Saxon church was replaced by the existing Norman building in 1100. The ashlar stone was from a local quarry and the flint was from the chalk down. There is a 13th-century Purbeck marble column in the north wall of the north transept. The organist has a squint into the chancel. The nave and north transept are Norman. The chancel is Decorated and the tower in two stages is 14th century. It has a crenellated battlement and the spire was rebuilt in 1853 using the original stone. This is a shorter version and has a lightning conductor.

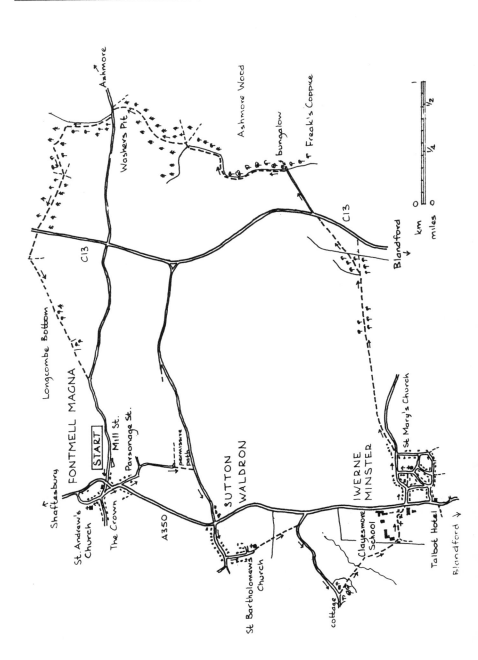

The Walk

Go along Mill Street for 300 metres to the main A350 and cross to the pub, the Crown opposite. This is the only pub I know which has a bridge over a brook and toilets on the other side. Continue past the pub and away from the main road. In 100 metres you come to a tree in the middle of a road junction. Turn right into Church Street and Fontmell Magna church is 100 metres ahead.

After visiting Fontmell Magna church, return to the tree and bear left to take the road signposted to Blandford Forum. This leads back to the A350. Cross with great care to Parsonage Street, diagonally to the right. Go past a plant nursery and follow the lane south-east as it dwindles to a path and veers south in a sunken way. When the right of way goes left uphill, keep straight on up into a field. This is a newly opened permissive path which goes south across the field with views to Hambledon Hill. At a tarmac lane turn right and walk down the lane to cross the main A350 to Sutton Waldron. Walk along 'The Street' through the centre of Sutton Waldron for 300 metres. Turn left along Church Lane.

After visiting Sutton Waldron church at the end of the lane, continue south-east across two fields down to a tarmac road. Turn right and walk up the road for 700 metres as far as a brick cottage in woodland. Take the driveway on the left. It becomes a farm track and goes diagonally down across two fields to Claycesmore School. Halfway across the second field, head for a group of sheds at the edge of the school grounds. Cross the stile and follow the driveway to the right along the side of playing fields. Follow signs and head east. Pass the church to come out at the main entrance. The war memorial of Iwerne Minster is on the right across the main A350.

Pass the war memorial, heading east into the village. Pass the village pump and in 15 metres there is a tarmac path signposted to the church.

For the bus back to Fontmell Magna, wait opposite the Talbot Hotel.

For the walk: After visiting Iwerne Minster church, turn right up Church Hill passing the end of the footpath. At the road T-junction turn right and in 140 metres, just past the next junction, there is a half-hidden bridleway signposted to Ashmore on the left. Turn up here and follow the wide, enclosed track uphill away from Iwerne Minster. There is a deep valley on the left. In nearly one mile at the start of a second wood, fork left on a grassy track. You can see the traffic of the busy C13 road ahead. Leave the woodland and, keep on course across the open field towards a gate to the C13. This is the higher Shaftesbury to Blandford road. Cross to the tarmac estate road opposite, through an avenue of beeches leading to Freak's Copse. Do not enter the wood but at a bungalow turn left. Follow the edge of the wood walking north for 500 metres. As the woodland recedes, you turn right and follow the edge down, sinking steeply into a remote green valley.

At the bottom only then do you enter Ashmore Wood. Inside are crosspaths. Turn left and follow the wide, level forestry track, which curves gently round, to Ashmore Road at Washers Pit.

Turn left along the road for 60 metres and turn right onto a signposted track, heading north between wire fences. The track veers left and starts gently climbing. At a break in the wire fence on the left, turn left and go fairly steeply uphill through woodland. Keep to the track heading west-south-west as far as a junction of tracks. Take the one half-right opposite which rises north-west back to the C13 road.

Cross to the footpath opposite through newly planted trees and, at cross tracks, keep straight on. You are soon on the edge of magnificent Longcombe Bottom. Bear left on a narrow descending path, which has been well trodden by walkers and deer. Go down through one copse and pass another at the bottom. Here you are approaching one of the many springs which merge at Springhead. A lovely garden has grown around the water here. Bear right and follow the tarmac road, which becomes Mill Street back to the riverside picnic site.

Walk 19

Compton Abbas – Ashmore – Melbury Abbas

This is quite a·challenging walk with hills and vales and long sweeping views. There is the additional adventure of an airfield to cross. Snacks can be had at the airport cafeteria.

Starting point: Compton Abbas church beside the A350; GR868184

Maps: Explorer 118 and Landranger 183, 184

Distance: 9 miles

Terrain: Hilly

The Churches

The name 'Compton' in Compton Abbas means 'farm in the valley' in Old English and the original church of St Mary was in the eastern, lower end of the village. Only the tower remains of that 14th-century thatched church.

Ashmore's little church has been rebuilt by the Victorians

The Victorians decided the old building was too dilapidated to repair and built a new church beside the new turnpike road, now A350. Much of the stone from the old church, together with local stone from a quarry at Whitehall near Shaftesbury, was used in the new building. This began in 1866. and was consecrated 16 months later – they did not let the grass grow under their feet! This is a handsome church with a slender tower and broach spire. Inside, the chancel and apse have stone rib vaulting. The font is Norman. The hassocks are embroidered with wild flowers, marking the centenary of the new church.

Ashmore's Saint Nicholas is another medieval church rebuilt by the Victorians. It is built of greensand stone and flint in 1874 in early Decorated style. Note the

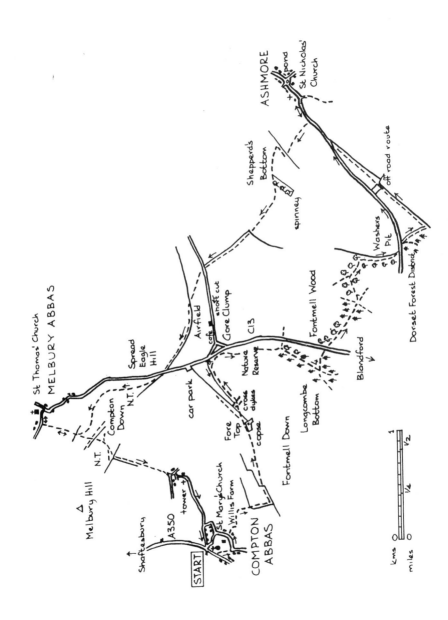

corbels, stones projecting from the wall near the roof. These are carved into the shapes of animals by John Skeaping in 1949 to illustrate Psalm 42, 'as pants the hart for cooling streams'. Ashmore is the highest village in Dorset. It is also most picturesque with a large village pond overlooked by fine stone cottages.

The first church would have been built in Melbury Abbas about 1000 years ago. 'Melbury' is a Saxon word meaning 'multi-coloured, fortified place'. The 'Abbas' links the village with Shaftesbury Abbey, which prospered until the Dissolution in 1538. The original church has been absorbed into the present structure of St Thomas, which was built in 1851 in Decorated style. The hidden rubble in the walls may have come from the old church. The new church has greensand stone outer layer. The stone came from a local quarry and is good quality ashlar. Light yellow Bath stone is used for windows and doorways. Stone foliage is carved on the arch of the south porch. The plinth of the ornate font is blue lias. There are many carvings inside and out. On the outside of the nave are carvings of kings, in Saxon style with beards and moustaches.

The Walk

From the church, go south down a tarmac track for 50 metres to a sign 'Willis Farm House'. Bear right here down a sunken lane to the village road. Turn left and walk along the road for 140 metres. Here the bridleway on the right, signposted to 'Gore Clump', heads for the hills. Follow the enclosed path around several bends to emerge into a field. In 130 metres you are offered a choice of paths. Avoid the path sharp left and continue ahead to the field corner. Here turn left and follow the boundary to find the National Trust sign at a gate in the corner. Keep climbing north-east up Fontmell Down and along Fore Top. Compton Abbas is below on the left and, far up ahead, you can see the traffic on the C13 road from Shaftesbury to Blandford. The Down expands as you climb, revealing steep bottoms where sheep could go over the edge. Look behind to see Blackmore Vale.

On Fontmell Down, the National Trust has provided extra paths, not shown on the OS map. 70 metres after passing a copse, cross the stile on your right. Head diagonally over the field to a fence corner and pass through cross dykes. Continue towards the C13 road. Deep cut Longcombe Bottom is below on the right. Just before the road at another copse, turn right. Keep the trees on your left and head down to enter the nature reserve. Here you take a narrow permissive path, which runs parallel to the road and overhangs Longcombe Bottom. In less than half a mile bear left to emerge onto a bridleway. Keep straight on, avoiding the path to the left. Continue for about 300 metres to crosspaths and turn left passing a strip of mainly fir trees. Shortly cross C13 road to the footpath opposite and enter Fontmell Wood.

Keep straight on heading south-east through the wood for less than half a mile. You come to a junction of several forestry tracks. Take the central one (opposite, half-left). There should be an arrow to point the way. Go fairly steeply downhill and in 300 metres, turn right at a T-junction. You have joined a secluded and enclosed track. In less than half a mile it brings you to a tarmac road. Here you have a choice:

Either:

The road: you can turn left and walk steadily up the road to Ashmore.

Or:

The path: you follow the high path, which runs parallel to the road. At the entrance to Dorset Forest District, take the second bridleway half-right uphill. At the top turn sharp left and go through a gate. Continue along the top of two long fields to rejoin the road to Ashmore. Just before you reach the village, on the left is the bridleway, which you will take later.

At Ashmore, visit the church on your left. Then go to the sizeable village pond with an interesting variety of stone cottages overlooking it. Return to the bridleway, on your right now. Head north-west on an enclosed grassy path. In 250 metres there is a kink in the path just before Shepperd's Bottom. Go down to the bottom, avoid the track to the right and keep close to the spinney on your left for 50 metres. Go uphill away from the spinney and keep north-west. In 600 metres you come to woodland and walk through the edge of the wood for a similar distance.

When you reach the tarmac road you may be tempted to turn left and take refreshments at the Compton Abbas Airfield cafeteria. You can also shorten the walk here by continuing on course then forking right back to the C13 road. Cross to the stile beside the copse opposite and you are back at the cross dykes of Fontmell Down. Retrace your steps to Compton Abbas.

Otherwise, cross Compton Abbas Airfield on the footpath. Choose your moment and run across the landing strip to the hedge on the other side. Turn left at the hedge and find the way through over a stile. After the stile turn left on a diverted path along the edge of the field. The hedge seems to give some protection from aircraft – probably an illusion. Melbury Abbas can be seen far below and downland beckons ahead.

Cross the C13 road at Spread Eagle Hill to National Trust land. Once inside, all is open and you can strike off to the right away from the track. Begin by going down parallel to the road on your right to reach an ancient earthwork. Melbury Abbas church can be seen below, straight ahead. Bear left along the high wide ledge around the down with scattered windswept hawthorn trees. Way below on your right you pass the church then the nearby Manor Farm. When the ledge dips, veer right and cross the main path from Melbury Hill. Avoid turning sharp right here but continue down to a gate in the hedge. Go through the gate, across a field to a tarmac lane and turn right for the church.

After visiting Melbury Abbas church, return along the lane and look south to the contour of Melbury Hill and Compton Down. There is a dip in the middle and this is your way back. Return over the field, back through the gate then start climbing the hill, heading for the dip. The peak and beacon of Melbury Hill is on your right. Go through a gate and keep heading south. You soon reach the other side. There is a wide rough track coming down from the left. Turn right onto this track and carry on downhill. In about 100 metres is a waymarked post. Here leave the track and bear half-left down the hill. Go out of the National Trust area through a gate. Bear slightly left through another gate and follow the field edge south with a hedge and fence on your right to join a farm track. Continue south towards the edge of Compton Abbas. Turn left at the farm and follow the road as it curves right and passes the remains of the old church of St Mary. Continue south-west on the village road for nearly half a mile. Just before the A350, turn half-left up steps and through trees to the church.

Walk 20
Edmondsham – Cranborne – Pentridge

This walk has Cranborne at the centre. It is possible to do the walk in two parts: From Edmondsham to Cranborne and back along leafy lanes and paths. Or, start the walk at Cranborne and head for the wide Celtic heights of Pentridge Down.

Starting points: Edmondsham village pump, GR066114, or the Sports ground, Penny's Lane, Cranborne, GR057134

Maps: Explorer 118 covers Cranborne to Pentridge, Outdoor Leisure 22 covers Edmondsham. Landranger 195 covers Edmondsham to Cranborne and Landranger 184 covers Pentridge

Distance: 12½ miles (can be shortened to 4½ or 9 miles)

Terrain: gently undulating to hilly

The Churches

Cranborne's church of St Mary and St Bartholomew was once the centre of an important town. Cranborne, taking its name from the little River Crane, had its own court, manor house, priory and market. In 930, Aylward Sneaw founded a Benedictine monastery here. There was already a college with six monks. At the time of Domesday 1086, the manor belonged to the Queen. Her son William Rufus gave it to Robert Fitz-Hammon who had already founded a monastery in Tewkesbury. In 1102, he moved the 120-year-old Abbey from Cranborne to Tewkesbury. Cranborne's ancient pulpit has initials 'T.P.' for Thomas Parker who was Abbot of Tewkesbury and Cranborne 1381-1421. Cranborne kept its important Priory until 1703 when it was demolished, a late victim of the Dissolution. The large church, built of stone and flint, has survived. There is an impressive Norman north doorway and an Early English nave. The barrel roof of the nave was repaired in1958. The chancel was rebuilt in 1875. The 13th-century font is of Purbeck stone. The massive tower is 15th century. The nearby manor house was built as a hunting lodge for Robert Cecil, Earl of Salisbury in 17th century. It is Jacobean in style and incorporates an earlier 14th-century building. Cranborne Chase, which spreads over downland in Dorset, Hampshire and Wiltshire, was the hunting ground of kings.

Edmondsham's St Nicholas is a small church which snuggles with the nearby 16th-century manor in a fold of clay countryside. The north arcade of the church is 12th century. The chancel arch and the tower are 14th century. The tower is of flint and greensand. The nave and chancel are brown sandstone. The manor gardens are often open to the public (Phone: 01725 517207).

In Pentridge, St Rumbold's is built of flint and stone blocks. Pentridge is a quiet hamlet below Pentridge Hill. The name in Celtic means 'hill of the boars'. St Rumbold was an 8th century saint. Sadly little is left of the ancient building. It was renovated by the Victorians. There is a short tower and a broach spire.

The Walk

Part 1

From the village pump, Edmondsham, take the wide straight track heading north-north-east, marked 'Bridleway to Cranborne'. In half a mile the main track curves right to a cottage. Here you turn left towards woodland. In about 400 metres take the footpath on the right down into the wood. This may be muddy in places. At the bottom you reach a T-junction and turn left on the track along the edge of the wood. Turn right down a tarmac lane and you soon emerge at the edge of Cranborne, by a recycling centre on the Alderholt Road. Turn right here then immediately left into Hibberds Field, a road with new houses. Bear left onto a path beside the stream, the River Crane and into Cranborne. You reach the new village hall and a school. Turn right on the Damerham Road. Penny's Lane is 50 metres on the right. _Follow Part 2 of the walk to visit Cranborne church._

To return to Edmondsham from Cranborne, go back along the River Crane to Hibberds Field. Cross to the lane to the left of the recycling centre. Go up this lane to the wood which you keep on your left. In 300 metres at the T-junction, turn left along the road to Edmondsham. Look across the fine woodland to the left. Ignore turnings to the right. In half a mile you pass the west entrance to Edmondsham House on the left and reach the pretty little Edmondsham church, also on the left. After visiting the church, continue on the Alderholt road through the village up to the pump and car park.

Part 2.

From Penny's Lane, cross with care to Grugs Lane opposite. At the end turn left, ignoring the bridleway to the right. Veer right for Cranborne church. From the church head, north to the corner of Swan Street near the little River Crane. There is a choice of paths here, both marked 'Jubilee Trail'. Avoid the one on the left and go forward north for 40 metres. Turn left on a well defined slightly elevated bridleway heading westwards at first. After crossing an avenue of beeches the path continues flanked by a newly planted row of trees and a hawthorne hedge. In 250 metres the path comes

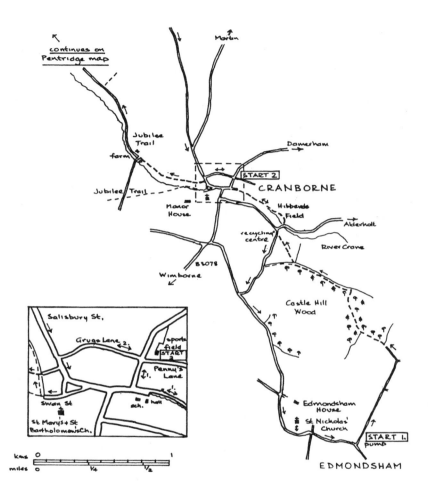

down to a farm at a tarmac farm lane. Keep north-west along the lane and ig-
nore the path on the right. In about half a mile at a farm, turn right, still on
Jubilee Trail. Climb up for half a mile to crosspaths, called Jack's Hedge
Corner and turn left. This track with hedges is still climbing on Jubilee
Trail. Ignore the path on the left and you reach Pentridge Hill in less than a
mile. Here the trail opens onto downland and you join Hardy Way.

Make for an elevated pine wood ahead and keep it on your right as you
continue north. Pentridge village can be seen below on the left. Cross a stile

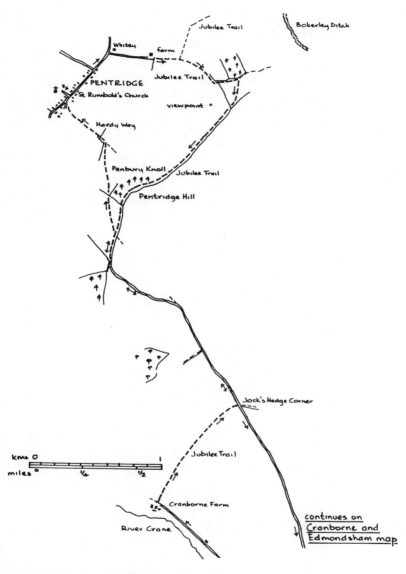

and bear half-left through scrub. When you are level with the church, at a fence corner, turn left downhill to follow Hardy Way down an enclosed path. At the bottom turn right along the village lane for 50 metres then left for Pentridge church.

From Pentridge church return to the village lane, turn left and walk to the end. Here at Whitey Top Farm, turn right and follow the stony track uphill, passing farm buildings on the left. Continue ahead uphill on a grassy track to join Jubilee Trail. Avoid the left branch of the trail which leads to Bokerley Ditch. Go right over a stile then straight on, curving around above woodland. At a signpost strike off sharp right up to a wonderful hilltop with views all around: Hampshire to the east, the coastal hills to the south and Wiltshire to the north and west. Continue walking along this magnificent ridge towards pine trees which form Penbury Knoll.

Follow the fence on the ridge and begin your descent. You soon find you are on familiar ground and retrace your steps to Jack's Hedge Corner. Avoid the turning to the right and keep straight on between hedges for one and a half miles back to Cranborne. You enter Cranborne by Salisbury Street. Keep going and turn left into Grugs Lane to return to the sports ground.

Trent's ancient church north-west of Sherbourne
has a fine tower and spire (Walk 22)

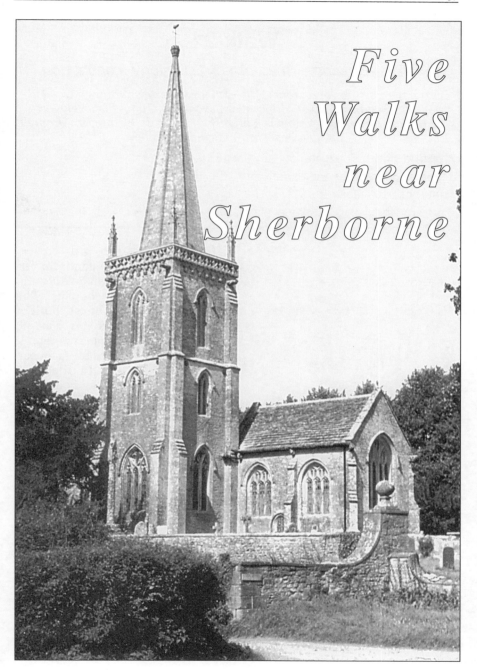

Five Walks near Sherborne

Walk 21

Folke – Haydon – Sherborne – Lillington – Longburton

From the pastures and crops of Blackmoor Vale down through wooded slopes to Sherborne Lake with castles beyond, and into this lovely town, dominated by the Abbey, this is a breath-taking walk. You return through pretty villages with ancient churches.

Starting point: Folke church; GR659133

Maps: Explorer 129 and Landranger 183, 194

Distance: 10 miles

Terrain: Undulating. Muddy in places.

The Churches

Sherbourne Abbey, considered the finest church in Dorset, is at the centre of the town

St Lawrence's stands in the quiet hamlet of Folke amid mellow stone houses. The nearby manor house, built of rubble stone, dates back to 1500. The church was rebuilt in 1628 in unusual Jacobean Gothic style. Inside, oak screens, bench ends and the communion rails are all Jacobean.

Sherborne Abbey, Church of the Blessed Virgin Mary, built of golden Ham Hill stone, is the most beautiful medieval church in Dorset. In AD 705 King Ine founded the see of Sherborne which stretched as far as Cornwall. St Aldhelm, a scholar and musician was the first bishop. He built a cathedral church. In AD 998 a Benedictine monastery was established here. In 1075 the bishopric moved to Old Sarum and later to

Salisbury. The monastery stayed in Sherborne. A flourishing medieval town developed and in the late 14th century a large church, All Hallows, was built at the west end of the Abbey for the townsfolk. In 1437 the parishioners, objecting to the removal of the Abbey font and to the narrowing of a west doorway, set up their own font. The Bishop of Salisbury intervened in the dispute but a parish priest shot a flaming arrow into the thatched part of the abbey roof and set it alight. The red stones in the pillars west of the tower are evidence today of this fire. The argument continued until Bishop Beauchamp, fearing for his life, consecrated the new font in All Hallows.

After the fire, building work went on apace. Abbot Bradford completed the choir and Abbot Ramsam (1475-1504) rebuilt the nave and remodelled the transepts. At the Dissolutiion, John Horsey sold the abbey to the town for £320. All Hallows was demolished in 1541 and the stone sold. The mainly 15th-century abbey still contains some Saxon work; a Saxon doorway with some long and short work is in the south wall of the west cloister, now the library of Sherborne School. The 15th-century fan vaulted stone roof of the nave and choir is exceptionally intricate and beautiful. Much of the Norman church, built by Bishop Roger of Caen in 1120, is incorporated in the abbey. The transepts and south porch are Norman. The famous disputed west doorway of 1430 is set into the round-headed Norman doorway.

The world has passed by Lillington, a rural part of Dorset. The church, St Martin's, a barn and a lake make a happy composition. This is a simple church with a late 13th-century nave and a Perpendicular tower. There is a plastered wagon roof.

In Longburton, the church of St James is next to the village pub on the A352. There are fields behind and in no way is the church jostled by traffic. The oldest part of the church is the Norman zigzag on the east of the north aisle. The tower is Early English. The nave and chancel are Perpendicular with a panelled chancel arch. The north chapel is Jacobean.

The Walk

Head north up Church Lane. Pass the road on the right and ignore the footpath to 'Wootton' at a bend in the lane. Just before a cottage on the left, turn right through a farm gate. This path takes you straight to Wootton on a higher and drier course. Follow the hedge on your right, crossing fields until you come to an enclosed grassy way, Clotfurlong Lane. This leads to the hamlet of North Wootton and the A3030. Cross the main road to a short path to the lane opposite and turn right up tarmac West Lane. As you leave the hamlet, you can see the remains of its church in a field on the left.

In about one mile you reach Haydon whose church has recently been converted into a private house. Turn left at the T-junction, pass the converted church on the right and you come to grand gates on the left. Ignore the 'No Entry' sign; this is a public footpath through the castle grounds. Follow the driveway straight on towards woodland, passing occasional deserted camp buildings and ignoring the unremarkable path to the right. About 100 metres inside the wood, you find large, corrugated farm buildings. The path leads behind the last of these monstrosities and continues through woodland before curving to the right and emerging into lovely parkland with scattered trees. Follow the track downhill. This opens to a grand view over the lake to Sherborne Castle.

As you draw closer, you realise that the old 12th-century castle is behind the new building of Walter Raleigh and the lake divides them. Capability Brown had the River Yeo flooded to make this lake. You cannot go down to the castles here. The path veers left uphill to a few trees, comes out of the castle grounds and follows the grassy slope above New Road at Sherborne. Cross the road and then the railway line into Sherborne.

After visiting Sherborne Abbey, return to New Road and turn right on the pavement. In about 250 metres, at the busy crossroads of Dancing Hill, take the road diagonally opposite, signposted to Thornford and Yetminster. You are now on the long distance footpath, the Macmillan Way, whose logo is 'Across Country For Cancer Care'. Follow the road as far as a bend and fork left up an enclosed track, muddy in winter and in no way conducive to dancing. You approach the A352 near the top of the hill then turn right below woodland. Macmillan Way skirts below the wood for about 300 metres before entering it and leading up to a tarmac lane. Turn right here, walking south-west with views over the hedge to distant hills. In less than one mile turn left at a fork in the road and go gently down to Lillington. This is where you leave Macmillan Way. The church can be found in a lovely dell with pond and willows. On the hill behind stands a folly.

The footpath to Longburton is signposted. Go past the church on a track, which dives to the right and then continues east towards a small wood. Keep this on your right and in 300 metres you find yourself next to St Anthony's College with a modern church and Leweston Manor with a stone chapel. If you wish to visit these, apply to the college. Then keep on the footpath with the school buildings on your right. At a crossways, turn left down the driveway for 100 metres. Turn right onto a footpath through young orchards. You are heading north-east. Cross a tarmac lane then fields keeping to the right-hand edge. You come out opposite the church and pub of Longburton.

To return from Longburton to Folke, take the driveway between the church and pub continuing north-east. In less than half a mile pass the delightful Jacobean manor, West Hall, on your right and a farm on your left. Cross the tarmac lane to a footpath diagonally to the left opposite and the mellow buildings of Folke are ahead. The manor here is a smaller version of West Hall.

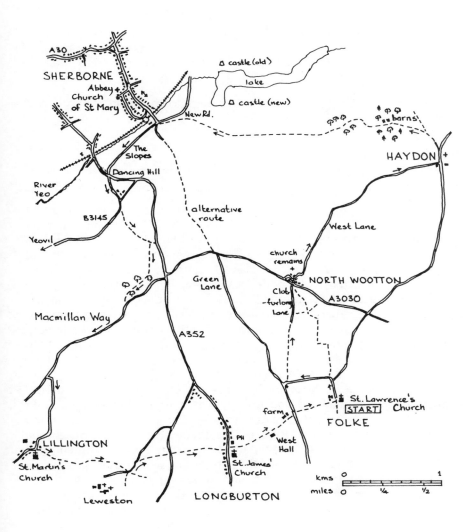

Walk 22

Trent – Nether Compton – Sandford Orcas

This walk takes us across peaceful hills close to the Somerset border. The ancient villages, with grey and yellow stone cottages, are sheltered from 21ˢᵗ century bustle. The churches reveal some of their chequered past.

Starting point: Trent church; GR590185

Maps: Explorer 129 (on the edge of this map, to be unfolded and turned over); Landranger 183

Distance: 9 miles

Terrain: Undulating. Muddy in places.

The Churches

St Andrew's, in Trent, is most fortunate to have an ancient spire, the gift of the Augustinian Priory of Studley, Warwickshire. The church is mainly 13ᵗʰ century with a fine early 14ᵗʰ-century tower. The chancel was rebuilt in 15ᵗʰ century in Perpendicular style. The east window has some pieces of medieval glass. The rood screen is also 15ᵗʰ century, as are the bench ends with carvings of birds, deer, a hound and others. Four have the inscription 'Ave Maria Gratia Plena Dominus Tecum'. Fearing the arrival of Cromwell and his distaste for Latin, the villagers removed the pews and muddled them. They have since been put in the right order again. Outside, the old cross is a peace memorial. The neighbouring chantry house was built 1440 with handsome, traceried windows. Behind the church is the manor where Charles II hid after the Battle of Worcester in 1651.

In Nether Compton, the main church of St Nicholas was built in the 13ᵗʰ century when the sheep and wool trade was thriving and landowners could afford to be generous. Sherborne Abbey owned the land of Nether Compton and monks agreed to the building of this chapel. Priests from Sherborne held mass here until 1405 when the first rector was appointed. The mid-14ᵗʰ-century plagues depleted the population, which must have recovered by the 15ᵗʰ century when the church was enlarged and a stone screen with five bays was also built. The screen is of fine medieval carving with tracery at the top. 500 years ago when the church was consecrated, several crosses were cut in the stones that had been splashed by water. One of these crosses inside a circle faces you as you enter by the south porch.

In Sandford Orcas, St Nicholas church and the Manor stand together, a perfect whole above the village at the northern end. The church is built of coursed rubble and Ham Hill stone. There are stone slates on the roof. The handsome 16th-century manor house is also of Ham Hill stone. The name 'Orcas' comes from Richard de Orescuiltz, Norman Lord of the Manor. In the church the 15th-century south or manor chapel has a fine oak panelled ceiling. The chancel was rebuilt in 14th century and contains some 13th-century work. The fluted font is early 13th century. The nave, tower and manor chapel are Perpendicular. The 15th-century oak screen below the tower may have come from Sherborne Abbey.

The Walk

Head for the nearby pub and take the footpath on the left. Go straight across the field for 200 metres until you reach a narrow tarmac lane. Turn right and go down the lane passing sewage works on the right. Just before Mill

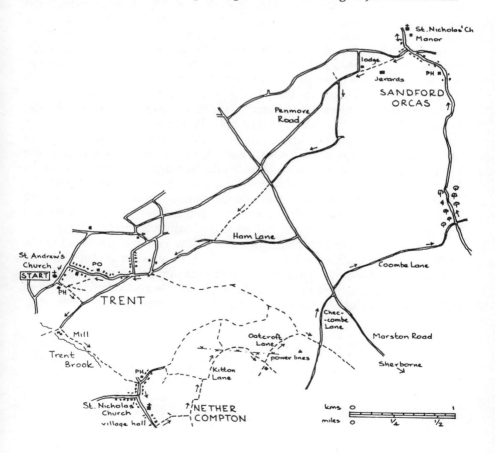

Farm at the bottom of the lane, turn left onto a bridleway that follows Trent Brook to Nether Compton half a mile away. When you emerge at Nether Compton, the pub is to the left. Turn right and walk along the village road to the church.

After visiting Nether Compton church, continue up the road to the village hall on the left. Do not turn into the driveway here. Instead, go up to the gate next to it. The footpath climbs gently up the grassy hill for 150 metres to a rough, hedge-lined track. Turn left and follow this track steadily uphill, ignoring paths to the left. Go under overhead cables and follow the track, known as Kitton Lane as it curves to the right. It goes under cables again and a steep little valley is on the right. When you reach a large barn at cross tracks, turn left into a narrow, hedge-lined Oatcroft Lane with the hill summit on the right. In 200 metres this curves down to a sunken footpath. Turn right onto the footpath and pass another barn on the left. At a crossways turn left onto a wide track, Checcombe Lane heading north. This leads to the main Marston Road. Cross with care to Coombe Lane opposite and walk north-east for nearly a mile to the Sandford Orcas Road. Turn left here and follow the road up through the village to the church at the northern end. This is a trek of over a mile but you do pass the pub on your way.

From Sandford Orcas church, return south down the village lane for 200 metres and take the first turning to the right, Penmore Road. This becomes a sunken way through a tree tunnel. Go past pillars at the entrance to Jerrards and turn left up steps to a footpath. This keeps to the right-hand edge of the field beside a row of trees with their trunks in a dip. The mellow stone of Jerrards is away to your left. You come out at an estate road and go past the lodge on your right to rejoin Penmore Road. Turn left along the lane then left again at the first track heading south between hedges. In half a mile at a T-junction of tracks, turn right and up to the main road half a mile away.

Cross with care to a footpath opposite. Below Yeovil can be seen in the distance. Head south-west following the hedge boundary on the right. At the end of this field go through a gap on the left into the next field and continue down on a path between ragged hedges. This leads to Ham Lane. Turn right, avoid the right fork and follow the lane to Trent.

Walk 23

Hinton St Mary – Marnhull – Sturminster Newton

The River Stour is never far away from this figure-of-eight walk with the pretty village of Hinton St Mary at the centre.

Starting point: Hinton St Mary church; GR787162
Maps: Explorer 129 and Landranger 183, 194
Distances: First part 4½ miles; second part 5½ miles
Terrain: Mainly flat, muddy in places.

The Churches

The church of St Peter stands close to the manor in a quiet, elevated part of the village of Hinton St Mary. The church was linked to Shaftesbury Abbey. The chancel has some 12th-and 13th-century stones. The font is 13th century. The Perpendicular tower still stands but the rest of the church was rebuilt in 1846. In the village, next to the forge, a large Roman mosaic was discovered. It is late fourth century and is believed to be evidence that Christianity had arrived in Dorset and was displacing Roman paganism. The mosaic includes the oldest known portrayal of the head of Christ. Pomegranates on either side of the head were symbols of immortality. In the same mosaic, Pegasus is depicted with Bellerophon on his back spearing the chimaera, a pagan depiction of the triumph of good over evil. The mosaic is now in the British Museum where it is to be given a prominent position in the Great Court. There should be a copy in the church.

St Gregory's is a large church on the southern edge of this sprawling village of Marnhull, at a sharp bend in the B3092. The glory of this church is its tall 15th-century tower with canopied niches, pinnacles and random bell openings. The 15th century has also left some treasures inside; the panelled wagon roof of the nave is beautifully formed and there are alabaster effigies of a husband and two wives on an altar tomb. The only Norman relic is a square pier in the north arcade. The church was restored in 1852 and again in 1882

In Sturminster Newton, John Selwood, Abbot of Glastonbury, built St

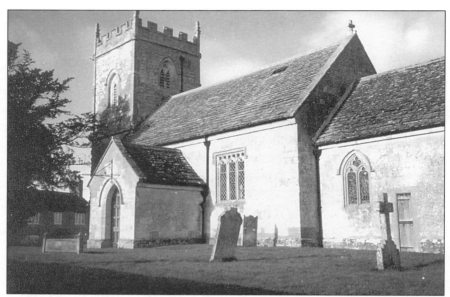

Hinton St Mary church, well restored, dates back to the 12th century. Christianity in this lovely village goes back to the 4th century; see Hinton St Mary Mosaic

Mary's in 1486. It replaces the earlier Saxon church. The monastery of Glastonbury had held the living of Sturminster Newton from AD 968, when it was a gift of King Edgar. Shaftesbury greensand stone, which is less inclined to weather than the local Marnhull limestone, was used inside and out. Fortunately the church was completed before the Dissolution of the monasteries in 1539. Sturminster or 'Stur' still has John Selwood's fine wagon roof with angels, a 15th-century tower and aisle arcades. Unfortunately another benefactor, Thomas Lane Fox, Curate and then Vicar of St Mary's, spent £40,000 of his own income in rebuilding and refurbishing in 1824. Chancel, transepts and porch are of this period. Greensand stone was again used for the outside.

The Walk

Part 1: From Hinton St Mary to Marnhull

From the church head for the nearby pub and turn right then left to join a path which emerges at the north-east corner of the village. At this corner step onto the firm track which goes down towards a plantation of trees. Follow the track as it curves right and walk with the trees on your left. The track ends at the north edge of the trees. Ignore the path to the right and continue north on a footpath over fields to sewage works which you pass on your right. Go through the tiny spinney to another field with a hedge on your right. At tarmac Eastwell Lane turn right then in 150 metres left onto a concrete track. This track leads to Marnhull but after 175 metres is no longer a right of way. There is a footpath to the left here across the field to crosspaths, take the path north to rejoin the concrete track at the top right-hand corner of the field. Continue north on the track through Church Farm and turn left at B3092. The pub and the church can be seen ahead.

After crossing the main road to Marnhull church, continue west down the suburban road. Pass a school on your right, keep straight on at crossroads. Turn left just past the village shop and a large house. *Some of the following footpaths have been numbered. Ignore the numbers as they do not apply to this walk.*

The footpath, signposted to Batt Alley and Walton House passes close to an arc of cottages, then opens onto a field. Take the right fork, go past the corner of a garden and turn left onto a driveway. You are now heading south past a bungalow and a house, 'Goddards Farm'. There is a pond with a seat on the right. Follow the footpath round the pond and into a field. Do not be tempted over to houses on the right. Instead, climb up the field with the hedge on your left and go through gates at a junction of hedges. In the next field you have the hedge on your right. Halfway, the hedge is replaced by a fence and you cross to the other side. Continue south with the fence on your left. Pass an old hedgerow on the left and go through a gap in the hedge in front. You are now in a larger field with the hedge on your right. This field ends with a curved corner and you can climb through to Mowes Lane.

Cross tarmac Mowes Lane to a concrete track and pass farm buildings of Antell's Farm. You reach a slurry pit and a mound. Keep these on your right and cross the field ahead down to the bottom left-hand corner where you can see a small copse. Go through the copse and follow the 'Hardy Way' sign heading south with a hedge on your left. Cross into the next field through the hedge and turn immediately right. In 75 metres cross another hedge and turn left. Below is the River Stour and ahead wide views over distant hills.

To return to Hinton St Mary, leave Hardy Way and turn left up a firm lane which passes a coal merchant. Then turn right along Marriage Lane and in 300 metres cross B3092 and head back to your starting point.

To continue to Sturminster Newton, turn right and follow the second paragraph of directions in Part 2 of this walk.

Part 2: Hinton St Mary to Sturminster Newton

Go to the nearby pub, turn right then left to the north-east corner of the vil-

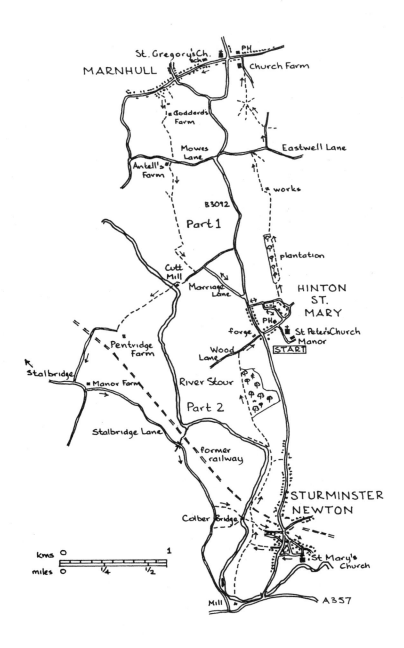

lage then turn left down to the main B3092. Turn right and cross to Marriage Lane diagonally opposite. In 300 metres turn left at a coal merchants.

Pick up Hardy Way, which leads down to the River Stour. Cross at Cutt Mill and take the footpath across meadows south-west to the lane at Pentridge Farm. This lane curves left and crosses the disused railway. In 450 metres you reach Stalbridge Road and turn left to Manor Farm 150 metres on the left. Here you join the tarmac track to the left. This is Stalbridge Lane, which narrows then widens again. After about one mile you turn left on a footpath across meadows and over Colber Bridge. This crosses the River Stour to Sturminster Newton, straight ahead.

After visiting the church and little town of Sturminster Newton, return along Church Lane, cross the busy Bridge Street to Ricketts Lane opposite to the right. This leads through playing fields to the river. Turn right and follow the riverside walk north, passing below the town on the right and through a broken railway bridge. Walk through newly planted trees, which form a nature reserve by the river. Do not be tempted to turn right up to the main road. Keep heading north across meadows towards woodland. Keep the wood on your right then cross the fields to Wood Lane. Turn right here and Hinton St Mary is 200 metres ahead. Cross the main B3092 to the lane opposite, which leads up to the church.

Walk 24

Iwerne Courtney (Shroton) – Child Okeford – (Hammoon)

Hambledon Hill, a prehistoric fort, 623 feet above sea level, is now a place of wildlife and dominates this walk. In Domesday, Shroton was 'sheriff's town' and the old name has survived today. The more recent 'Iwerne', from the river of that name, is pronounced 'youern'.

Starting point: Iwerne Courtney church; GR860124

Maps: Explorer 118 (does not include Hammoon). Landranger 194. Explorer 129 shows Hammoon but not the other villages

Distances: 3½ miles or 9 miles to include Hammoon.

Terrain: Hilly. One steep descent the rest is flat and may be muddy.

The Churches

Up to the First World War, Iwerne Courtney's Shroton Fair was almost as big as that of Woodbury Hill. (See *Bere Regis walk* under Wareham.) The Perpendicular church of St Mary was enlarged in 1610 and Gothic windows were put in the north aisle chapel and east bay of the south aisle. The east window is Victorian. This church was used as a prison in 1645. 'Clubmen' from the village and surrounding countryside were tired of religious conflict and determined to take on Oliver Cromwell's army. Sadly they were defeated and imprisoned in Shroton church. Today Shroton Churchyard is known to harbour 150 species of lichen.

In Child Okeford, the church of St Nicholas has a Perpendicular tower of greensand. The rest of the building is Victorian with bands of flint and stone. Sir Arthur Sullivan stayed at nearby Hanford House and attended this church. The inside is spacious. The walls of the chancel are faced with pinkish brown marble. Was there an earlier church here? Two windmills at 'Ackford' are mentioned in Domesday. The 13th-century Purbeck stone font has recently been moved to the south-west corner.

St Paul's in Hammoon is 13th century in origin. It is built of local Marnhull stone and green sandstone from Shaftesbury. In 1885, when the church was restored, Bath stone was also used. The church is on slightly raised ground and apparently in no danger of flooding from the nearby River Stour for in 1945 the chancel floor was lowered to its 15th-century level. Two pieces of 13th-century tile were discovered then and are now set in the west wall. The chancel is paved with Marnhull stone. The chancel windows are Early English. The sanctuary floor is of Purbeck stone. There is a 13th-century priest's door north in the chancel. In the 15th century the

Hammoon church is close to a handsome 16th-century manor

north wall of the nave was moved and two windows added. This made the nave narrower and explains why it is out of line with the chancel. Also added in 15th century were the porch and the exceptionally fine panelled timber roof on the nave. The reredos of Ham Hill stone was discovered in a scrap yard in London. Nearby Hammoon Manor is a 16th-century thatched house of well cut ashlar from Marnhull with a fine classical porch in Purbeck limestone.

The Walk

Part 1: Iwerne Courtney to Child Okeford.

From Iwerne Courtney church, head north along the road towards the pub. Do not go as far as the pub. Take the first turning left towards the cricket ground below Hambledon Hill. A bridleway on the left leads from the cricket ground. Follow it behind big old barns and the church, hidden among trees. In 200 metres, at a Y-junction, turn sharp right and follow the bridleway westwards up Hambledon Hill for half a mile to the old trig. point. Turn right towards the spectacular prehistoric earthworks. Keep these on your right and take the narrow path on the edge of the hill with magnificent views to the west. Child Okeford is the nearest village below. Pass above the manor house and church. After about half a mile walking

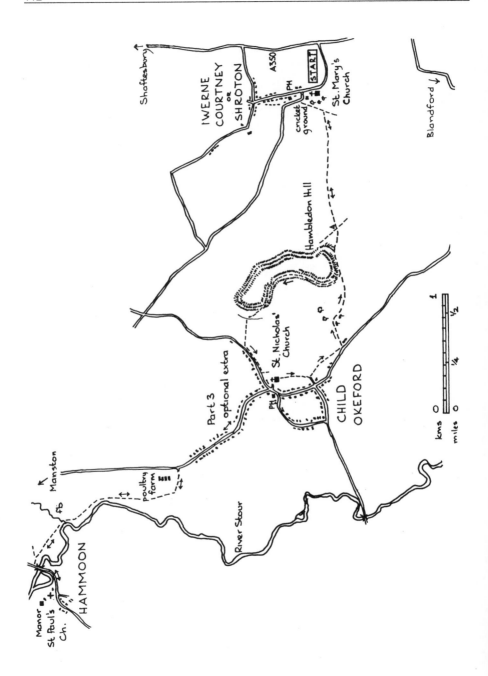

along the edge, you come to a steep descent to the village on the left. At the bottom turn right and in 50 metres you realise you have been in a nature reserve with a descriptive notice. Turn left out of the reserve and through a tree-lined path. When you reach the road, turn left for Child Okeford church.

Part 2: Child Okeford to Iwerne Courtney.

From Child Okeford church, go past the wooden arch in the churchyard. Steps in the churchyard wall lead to the footpath south over a meadow. Hug the fence on your right for about 150 metres. At the fence corner veer right towards a new detached house. Go through a farm gate and cross a wide track to the footpath diagonally to the right opposite. This enclosed path has trees on the right, meadows on the left. It leads south-east for about 200 metres. It joins the road at a point where it also meets the bridleway to Hambledon Hill. Turn left away from the road and onto this clear track back up Hambledon Hill. You come out near the trig. point and carry on east back to Iwerne Courtney via the track which brought you here.

Part 3: Child Okeford to Hammoon and back.

If the river has not flooded, the crops are not overwhelming and luck is on your side, this should be a pleasant riverside extension to the walk.

From the crossroads near Child Okeford church, take to road to Gillingham and Manston. In over half a mile you see a huge poultry farm looming ahead. Before you reach it, turn left down a track which may not be marked but is a public footpath. It emerges at a field. Turn right and follow the route north with a hedgerow on your right. In about 300 metres you reach the River Stour. Keeping it on your left, go through a gap and head for the field boundary opposite. Find and cross a well-concealed wooden bridge over a tributary of the river, not the rickety metal and concrete structure. Again approach the main river and follow the slight indentation in the ground across meadowland to the tarmac lane. Turn left, cross the river and Hammoon church is 300 metres away. The manor is just beyond the church.

From Hammoon retrace your steps to Child Okeford then follow Part 2 of the walk.

Walk 25

Hazelbury Bryan (Droop) – Pulham – Mappowder

This walk between unspoilt churches in the Blackmoor Vale should appeal to keen map readers. I met one local lady in Mappowder who told me she had never managed to find the way to Pulham. Dorset County Council is coming to the rescue with its new way-marking scheme. These notes should also help but an Explorer map, a compass, a stout pair of boots and a spirit of adventure are also valuable assets.

Starting point: Hazelbury Bryan Church, Droop; GR753083.

Maps: Explorer 117 Landranger 194

Distance: 10 miles

Terrain: Grazing land which may be very muddy in places. Few hills.

The Churches

The present building St Mary and St James, in Hazelbury Bryan, of roughly coursed rubble with ashlar dressings is a good example of early 15th-century architecture. The village is a scattered community; Kingston, Wonston and Droop have existed since the 7th and 8th centuries. The Plagues of 1348 and 1361 caused people to move from one area and settle in another. This could account for the church being so far from the main population. After the second Plague, there was a boom in church building. Lady Alice de Bryan is thought to be responsible for much of the excellent work in this church. During this period the tower, one of the finest in the Blackmoor Vale, was built, the nave was lengthened and the north aisle, including Perpendicular windows, was added. Lady Alice died in 1435, happy we hope in her achievements. Later in the century the additions of the south aisle and south arcade were less skilfully worked. The nave and north aisle have wagon roofs. The south aisle, south chapel and south porch have ceilings with moulded beams. The font is 12th century. The church was well restored in the 1930's and the chancel repaved with Purbeck stone. The original gargoyles, weathered though they are, still show the humour and fun the masons had in making them grotesque.

St Thomas Becket church and the 18th-century rectory stand remote from the village of Pulham. 'Poleham' was the name given in Doomsday. The land was shared between Rainbald the Priest and William de Moion who came to England with William the Conqueror. The present church is cruciform, the aisles are late additions. Tower, chancel and porch are Perpendicular. The chancel arch has two carved heads. There is a room with a

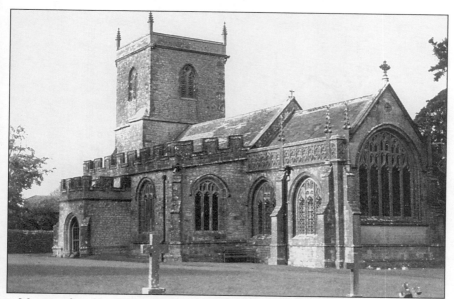

Mappowder church is a lovely, light Perpendicular building, a delight to visit

chimney above the porch. Priests from Milton Abbey would stay there. The canons, who held court in nearby Cannings Court Farm may also have attended this church. There are several gargoyles; one of a winged lion, another of a fish with a man on its head.

St Peter and St Paul is in Mappowder. 'Mapuldor' in Anglo-Saxon means 'maple tree' and reminds us that until 1279 this was the edge of the royal forest. Deer, wild boar, wild cats and even wolves roamed here. There were restrictions forbidding bows and arrows and tree felling. King John had a hunting lodge, which was later part of Mappowder Court, home of the Coker family. Medieval fairs were held at Mappowder for 12 days at the end of August. In the church, the 12th-century corbel heads, the font and a 14th-century effigy in Caen stone of a knight are witness of those far off days. The present building is consistently Perpendicular, late 15th or early 16th century, with battlements to the south. It is built of squared and coursed rubble with ashlar dressings of limestone and greensand. It was well restored by the Victorians and is light and spacious.

The Walk

From Hazelbury Bryan church at Droop, cross to the school and then to the footpath opposite. This heads south-west uphill towards a clump of trees.

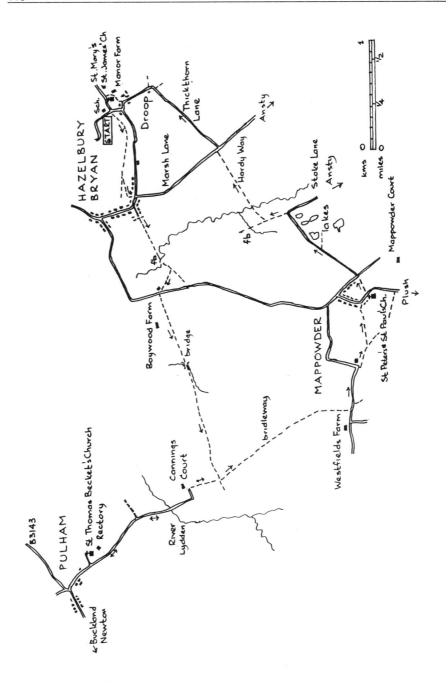

There are fine views. Go through the trees and cross the next field diagonally to a farm gate and enter the next long, sloping field. The first houses of Hazelbury Bryan can be seen on the left. Go past these and aim for the bottom left-hand corner of this long field. A narrow path here leads through to a road junction. Sherborne is signposted to the right. Turn right but only walk about 50 metres in this direction. Turn left at a post box into a no through road, passing a thatched cottage and some new houses to a footpath.

Follow the direction of the arrow south-west across fields for 350 metres down to a footbridge over a stream on the left and keep on course for 75 metres to a stile. Cross to a wide field and veer right towards a barn with Boywood Farm beyond. You should come to a gate onto a tarmac lane. Cross to the footpath hidden in the hedge opposite. Head south-west with the hedge on your right. Boywood Farm is on the other side of the hedge. Do not be tempted over any stiles on the right. In 350 metres cross farmgate to the next field and keep on course even though the hedge boundary bulges to the right. A little stream joins the footpath on the right. In about 100 metres, cross the bridge and walk with the stream on the left. Keeping south-west you then have to find the crossing through the hedge and over a ditch. Go across the next field and negotiate another hedge and ditch to arrive in a big field with a pond on the left. In less than half a mile you are faced by a bank on the other side of the fence.

Turn right here through the farmgate and into a muddy lane. You are now heading north to Cannings Court, named after the Canons of the church who lived here once. At this building turn left then right following the lane north, crossing the bridge over the tiny River Lydden and continuing between hedges. Avoid turnings to left and right for over half a mile. Pass the Old Rectory through trees on the right and turn right for Pulham church.

From Pulham church return down the long lane which brought you here and go past Cannings Court again. When you reach the field with the bank, now on your right, keep straight on. This bridleway is signposted when you reach the gate on the south side of the field. Keep to the bridleway going south-east for nearly one mile. In the next field keep straight on over the slight hillock to find the stile through the hedge. You now have a view down to buildings on the Mappowder Road. You need to head to the left of Westfields Farm. As you approach the farm, veer left over to the field boundary and follow the hedge to the tarmac road. If you have time from compass and map reading, do look up to admire the views of little hills on the fringes of Blackmoor Vale.

Turn left along the tarmac lane for 350 metres until you are opposite a large barn. The lane turns sharp left here. Mappowder church can be seen ahead. Turn right onto a track then immediately left onto a footpath beside the barn. You are heading south-east across fields and hugging the field boundary on the left. In 150 metres, turn left over a stile and into the field up to Mappowder. The footpath climbs the hillock and heads north-east. It does not go directly to the church but passes it and enters the village via a farm gate and along a track between houses. When you reach the village lane, the church is on your right.

From Mappowder church cross the lane to the footpath opposite heading north-east across a field for 150 metres. You come to a corner of a tarmac lane. (Mappowder Court is down the track to the right. See church note above.) You continue north-east on the lane. After 300 metres, through the hedge on your right, you catch glimpses of lakes and sometimes people fishing. Ignore the path to the right. In another 200 metres the lane bends right. Look for the bridleway in the left corner. Turn left and north. Ahead is an impressive new footbridge. This is not for us. We turn right just before the bridge and go gently uphill heading north-east on 'Hardy Way'. Although clearly defined, the way is muddy especially after fields when it is enclosed by trees and undergrowth.

Struggle up Hardy Way to the welcome tarmac of Marsh Lane. Turn right then left up Thickthorn Lane for half a mile. As it curves left at the top of the hill, you will be relieved to see the church ahead. You may even see the logic for Hazelbury Bryan church to be in Droop. After the curve in Thickthorn Lane you are now heading north-west for 200 metres to another bend. Here you can turn right onto a path through a private driveway with Manor Farm ahead, the village pond below and the church beyond. No rural scene could be more beautiful.

View from Tyneham towards Lulworth Cove and Portland (Walk 29)

_Five Walks
near
Wareham_

Walk 26

Wareham Town and River Walk

We visit two ancient churches, Lady St Mary on the south side of Wareham near the River Frome and St Martin on the north side, not far from the River Piddle. Both rivers enter Poole Harbour and Wareham was once a major port. After the Danes came to attack in 876, King Alfred made the town a fortified burgh with walls to keep them out. Both walks described here take us along the walls. The longer walk also follows the course of the rivers and is likely to be muddy. Rare breeding birds, water voles and even otters may be seen on the longer walk.

Starting point: The Quay at the lower, south side of Wareham; GR925872

Maps: Ourdoor Leisure 15 and Landranger 195

Distance: Short Walk 1 mile; longer Walk 4 miles

Local Information: The Tourist Information Office opposite the Quay offers a free leaflet about the rivers; 'The Wareham Royalty' is produced by the Environment Agency.

Terrain: mainly flat, the longer walk can be wet in the winter and possibly overgrown in the summer.

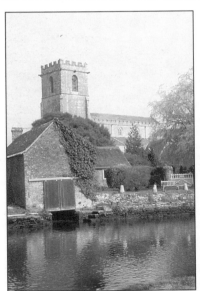
Lady St Mary, Wareham

The Churches

The Church of Lady St Mary stands in south-east Wareham near the River Frome. It is a landmark for sailors and road users. Inside this lofty building, you are aware of its importance. It was once a Benedictine priory church and was the minster for a wide parish. The large Saxon building, possibly the largest surviving in the country, lasted until 1842 when the Victorians rebuilt the nave and roof. They also introduced an efficient central heating system, still in use, with square pipes. Another Victorian addition is the coloured glass in the huge east window, built in 1325. There is an early 15th-century window in the south wall. Fortunately, the Victorians did not touch the charming St Edward's chapel with Norman entrance and 14th-century arch above. Here the ribs of the vaulted roof are of Purbeck stone. Do not miss the unique 12th-century lead font. Preserved in the church are engraved stones which date back to the 6th or 7th century. The languages on these stones are Welsh and Latin. They indicate that Celtic Christians took over a Pagan Roman temple. Welsh was the language of Purbeck even after the the Saxons came in AD 490.

The Church of St Martin-on-the-Walls, Wareham is one of the oldest churches in Dorset. The typically Saxon, tall narrow nave and chancel have 'long and short' stone work. The chancel arch is Norman. The north aisle was added in 1200. The wall paintings in the chancel are 12th century. They portray St Martin of Tours riding a horse and dividing his cloak to give half to a naked beggar. The colour red, used in these medieval frescoes, is taken from stones at nearby Red Cliff beside the River Frome. The south window in the nave is 14th century, the east windows in the nave and chancel are 15th century. The saddle back tower was added in 16th century. His brother gave the large, recumbent stone effigy of Lawrence of Arabia in 1939.

The Walks

Short Walk

Follow the well-marked 'Walls Walk' which leads behind Lady St Mary for 200 metres. At T-junction turn left and onto the road past houses. The Walls Walk then takes you up onto the grassy bank at the eastern edge of town. You cross minor roads leading out of town. In about 300 metres the Walls Walk leads away from houses to the north-east corner of the town. **The longer walk joins here.** The River Piddle is in view now. Follow the path as it curves left then brings you down into the north side of the town. Take the road on the left, still marked 'Walls Walk' and 50 metres on the right, you come to Lady's Walk to St Martin's Church.

Longer Walk (may be muddy)

Follow the 'Walls Walk' as far as the T-junction then turn right. The path veers left at a pump house then right across fields to the river. Turn left and follow the course of the river south-east for nearly half a mile. Opposite the bend is Red Cliff, which provided the red for the frescoes in St Martin's Church. From here the river winds mainly north-east for 1 mile. There are pleasure craft moored on the other side. Our side is the haunt of wild fowl. Pass Swineham Farm, seen across a field on the left.

In another 300 metres you cross a culvert and come to a track at a T-junction. *It is possible to shorten the walk here by turning left and follow-*

ing the track, which joins tarmac Bestwall Road back to Wareham one mile away.

More exciting is to turn right at the T-junction and towards Wareham Channel. Here are acres of reed beds, a bird watcher's paradise. Take care to follow the marked footpath. In 75 metres this turns left and heads north between hedges. In 250 metres the path veers left, right then left to the grasslands of the River Piddle.

Keep the hedge on your left and the banks of the River Piddle can be seen across the expanse of grassland to your right. In about 350 metres you reach woodland and veer right. You now keep this strip of woodland and a watercourse on your left. In 250 metres, cross the stile on the left into the wood. Here you follow the track enclosed with trees. Pass North Bestwall Farm on the left and go along a shady road for half a mile to the Town Walls. The road curves to the left and you scramble up the pebble path to the grassy walls and turn right. Continue as for the short walk.

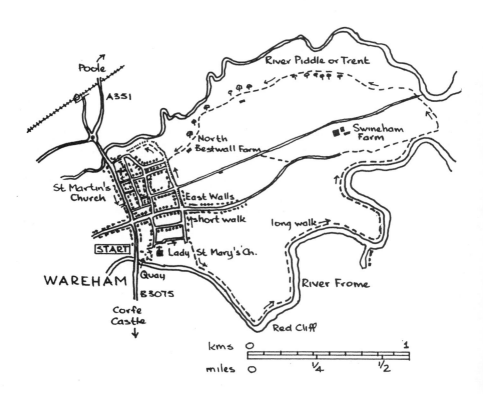

Walk 27

Corfe Castle – Studland – Swanage

From the spectacular hilltop castle ruins, this walk mounts the hills of the Isle of Purbeck. Not a true island, Purbeck has boundaries formed by the River Frome to the north, Poole Harbour to the east, the sea to the south and a little stream, Luckford Lake to the west. We walk the length of the hills over to the chalk cliffs of Studland to a delightful, Norman church. Then take the cliff walk to the seaside town of Swanage. The return from Swanage to Corfe is by steam train with refreshments on board or by bus.

Starting point: Challow Farm Car Park, Sandy Hill Lane, east side of Corfe Castle; GR964822

Maps: Outdoor Leisure 15 and Landranger 195

Public transport: steam train or bus 142 run quite frequently from Swanage to Corfe Castle. For more details phone Swanage Railway 01929 425800 or Wilts and Dorset Buses 01202 673555.

Distance: 10 miles

Terrain: hilly

The Churches

In Corfe Castle, the Church of St Edward, King and Martyr was built in the 13th century when Corfe was the centre of the Purbeck stone and marble industry. Purbeck stone was brought by horse drawn sledges to stone masons in West Street. Nearly the whole picturesque village is built of grey Purbeck stone. The church is believed to be sited near the spot where the body of young King Edward was found. He was murdered in 978 in the Saxon lodge, which was replaced by a Norman castle. His step-mother, Queen Elfrida ordered this crime so that her own son should become king. He was Ethelred, the Unready. The castle was extended by King John in 12th –13th centuries and courageously defended by Lady Bankes in 1646 in the Civil War. The Roundheads maltreated the church, using it as a base from which to bombard the castle. A canon was set on the church tower. A traitor in the castle opened the gates to the Roundheads who tried and failed to demolish the castle. The Bankes family continued to own the castle and it was given to the National Trust in 1981. The 15th-century church tower, built of Ashlar, withstood the onslaught and stands firm today. The 20th century is taking good care of the tower with its fine gargoyles. The whole bowl of the 14th-century marble font, used as a drinking trough by horses of the Roundheads, now stands under the tower arch. In 1859 the rest of the

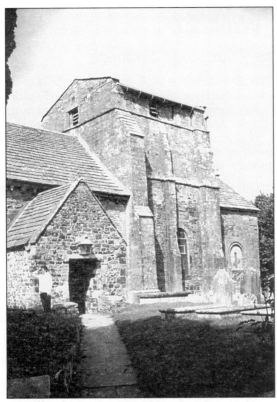

Studland is a strong Norman church near the coast, north of Swanage

church was rebuilt in Gothic style using original stonework where possible. The Purbeck marble pillars in front of the altar are replicas of those of the former building. Some archways in the chancel are original 13th century. Outside on the east gable of the church stands a small statue by Francis H. Newbery of St Edward, King and Martyr.

The Congregational Chapel built 1835 has a pleasant aspect on the green next to Corfe Common where 100 species of wild flowers bloom.

The sturdy Norman church of St Nicholas has stood for 1000 years in Studland. Close to the coast, it is buffeted by winter blasts, washed by spring rains and bleached by summer suns. An earlier Saxon church, believed to have been built by St Aldhelm in the 7th century, was vandalised by the Danes. They were defeated by King Alfred in 877. Saxon work can be seen inside, in the rubble north wall and outside in the chancel walls. The vaulted roofs of the tower and sanctuary and the Norman arches of the chancel are impressive. The groins in the roof are made of Purbeck 'Burr', a stone from Swanage which can only be seen at low tide. There are Norman windows in the north walls. The Early English east window is simple. The building of the tower ended before it reached full height. Even so, it was found necessary to add buttresses in the 13th and 14th centuries. The porch and gallery are 18th century. Preservation work started in 1880 uncovered flint cists, both Christian and pre-Christian, suggesting a church built on the site of a heathen temple. The carved heads under the eaves are a puzzling assortment of animal and human grotesque figures. Easier to understand is the dedication; St Nicholas was guardian of sailors.

St Mary's, in Swanage, is a large church with 14th-century tower. The rest is mainly Victorian. A transept window shows St Aldhelm with staff and mitre and Bishop Jewell with book.

The Methodist church, built in 1886 on the slope above the Parish Church, has recently been refurbished inside. The octagonal steeple is part of the skyline of Swanage.

The Walk

Follow signposted Purbeck Way up onto the ridge. In 200 metres the path forks, the right-hand route takes a lower course, underhill and often muddy. I recommend the higher path on the left as it leads to views over Poole Harbour and beyond. This wide path is a joy to follow along well drained, cropped grass. Milestones indicate Ulwell about three and a half miles distant. Halfway, we go across Ailwood Down with many tumuli and one long barrow. After passing a trig point on the left, the path veers right, downhill and converges with the lower path. Keep going downhill. Follow the hard track and avoid turning right to Ulwell. The road can be seen ahead. Just before the road, turn left off the track. At the road turn left for the footpath diagonally opposite. Do not be alarmed, this does not go up the steep hill. It veers right towards the Coastal Path. You are on a rough track above Ulwell Farm. In 250 metres at crosspaths, the obilisk is marked to the left. We ignore this and continue on the rough path, which skirts the hill for half a mile. It becomes a narrow footpath. At crosspaths Studland is indicated. Turn left and follow this path uphill, heading north-east and passing several stone benches on the way. The bench at the top has the motto, partly erased: 'Rest and be thankful'. Continue on route down an estate road past houses on the left. Studland can be seen ahead. You arrive there at cross tracks. At a farm on the left, teas and light lunches are served. Pass Studland Cross on the green on the right and follow the road marked 'The Church Only'.

After visiting Studland church, return to the Cross and turn left along the lane towards the coast. At a bend in the road there are public toilets which you pass on your left as you turn right onto the South West Coast Path towards 'Old Harry'. He and his wife, together with a natural arch, are rock formations in the sea below the cliffs at Handfast Point. From the Point, the path turns right following the coast south-west. At Ballard Point the path veers right and begins a gradual descent but there is some cliff erosian here. It is possible to take a more inland route by going through a gate on the right and entering a fenced area with a trig point on top. In half a mile the Coast Path joins the fenced route. Swanage can be seen below. Follow the coastal path down and in half a mile you have to turn right and make your way first through a bungalow estate then through hotels and

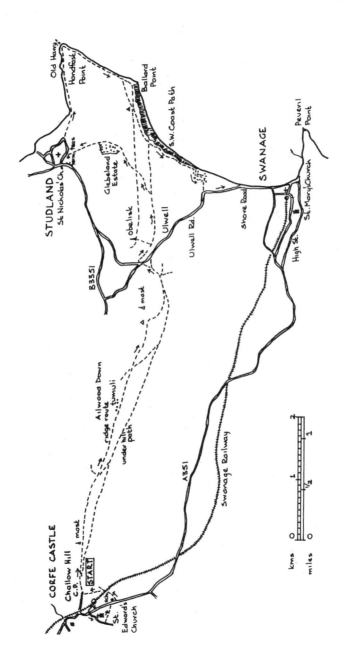

guest houses. At the main road turn left and continue downhill to Shore Road. Keep going to the town and beach. The steam railway is indicated to the right. Just beyond it, stands St Mary's Church. The steam train offers a delightful journey with refreshments back to Corfe Castle.

From Corfe Castle station, visit the church then go down the steps below the tower. Turn left along West Street for 75 metres then turn left along a passage to a recreation ground. Across the green is the Congregational Chapel. Go past the chapel with its pretty garden and emerge onto A351. Turn right and go past the village school to a footpath sign on left. The path crosses a field then the railway line. It crosses a footbridge into the next field. Cross the field diagonally left heading for Challow Farm. Come out at the farm gate, turn left on the tarmac lane and Challow Farm Car Park is on the right.

Walk 28

Winterborne Whitechurch – Bere Regis

From a rugged rural church across gentle downland, we visit an important centre for Royalty in bygone days.

Starting point: Winterborne Whitechurch Church; GR836001

Maps: Explorer 117 and Landranger 194

Distance: 7 miles

Terrain: undulating

The Churches

In Winterborne Whitechurch, St Mary's stands at the lower end of Chescombe Lane opposite the mellow brick vicarage of 1743. The church may owe its names to its white stones and flint. These are in alternate courses in the tower. Inside, the church is spacious and welcoming with a burning lamp in the Lady Chapel. The sturdy 12th-century pillars of the tower come between nave and chancel. Winged angels' heads on the capitals are full of character. Some of the colourful stencilling over the tower arches is medieval, the rest is the work of the vicar's wife in 1882. The chancel with windows and arch is Early English. There is an intricate 15th-century font and a colourful pulpit of the same period. The pulpit is from Milton Abbey. It was plastered over to hide the carvings of the four Evangelists from Oliver Cromwell's mob. In 1867, thought to be of no value, it was given to Whitechurch. Two years later the plaster was removed revealing its true worth. Outside, built into the north wall is a rough cross which may be Saxon. The tower is Perpendicular.

St John Baptist is in Bere Regis and, as the name suggests, royalty visited this town. In 978, Queen Elfrida, stepmother of the murdered King Edward the Martyr, moved into the manor east of the church, now Court Green. King John also had a manor here, 1204-1216. Later lords of the manor in the 13th century were the Turbevilles. Thomas Hardy adapted this name for his novel, Tess of the D'Urbervilles. Fires have destroyed many old buildings of Bere Regis. The stone church alone stands witness to ages past. The 12th-century arcade was once attached to an earlier building here. The capitals of the arcade have original carvings by a mason who has amused generations of church goers. He depicts a man with a toothache, a headache, a monkey's head and a king's head. The finely carved font is also Norman. The north aisle was added 50 years later. In 13th century the aisles were extended and flint walling of the period can be seen outside at the west end of the north aisle. The local brown heathstone in the south doorway and in the east arch of the arcade is 14th century. The chancel was refaced with ashlar in 15th century. Most remarkable of all is the 15th-century oak roof with large carved figures of the 12 Apostles looking down on the congregation. The imposing 16th-century tower is of chequered flint and Purbeck stone, also including local brown heathstone.

The Walk

Cross the nearby A354 to the quiet road opposite, Rook Lane. This follows the course of the River Winterborne, the stream on the left. Head south on this road for one mile, past the occasional thatched cottage. Ignore the farmtrack on the left and the footpath on the right. Just before a farm on the left, the road curves left and you turn right through a double metal farm gate. Take the wide straight footpath ahead, which continues in a southerly direction up to a small plantation on West Down. The countryside stretches far and wide with open fields, few trees and just the occasional distant copse. Go through a narrow way at the top and continue south on a path to cross tracks. The track on the left leads to Winterborne Kingston. We keep straight on along a farm track. We have joined Jubilee Trail. For half a mile this is wide and flat. The track bears left at a farm and we keep straight on along a bumpy, grassy way for 300 metres then descend to the A35. Cross with care to the path opposite. This brings you to a quiet part of Bere Regis. At the T-junction in the town, turn left. Go past the post

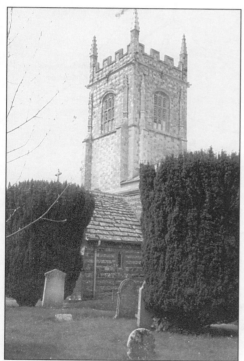

Bere Regis has an ancient church with a handsome tower. There is much history, architecture and humour here. See the church notes for this walk

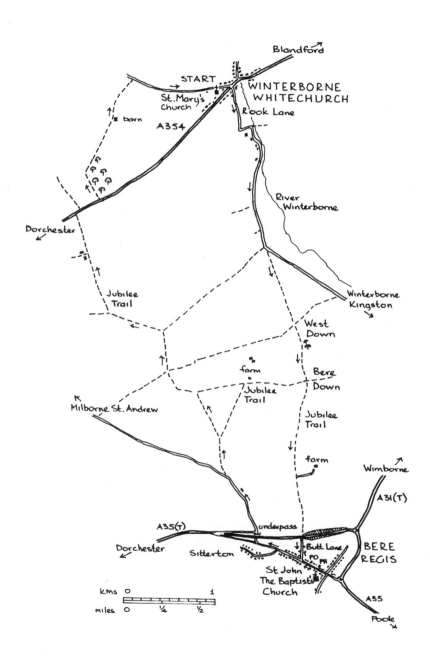

office, shops and pub on the left. The church is 100 metres down on the right.

For the return walk, go back past the post office, shops and pub and ignore the track which brought you here. Instead, carry on past Butt Lane on the right and the turning to Sitterton on the left. (This is a hamlet with thatched cottages). You are heading for the A35 again. Take the underpass on the right, marked to Milborne St Andrew. Follow this road for 300 metres then turn right up a wide farm track. In 200 metres the track veers right to farm buildings which can be seen ahead. You turn left up a bridleway with an easily missed blue waymark on the left. You are heading north with the hedge on the right.

When you can no further on this route, you join Jubilee Trail which has come up from the right. Follow the markers for Jubilee Trail heading north-west. You can make out the road to Milborne St Andrew below on the left whenever a lorry passes. A hedge is on your right again. Ignore crosspaths and a also a path to the right.The hedge has thickened. Go down for another 250 metres until you reach a narrow path on the right. This goes through a strip of woodland scrub and emerges at a lane with a large house on the left. Follow the lane north. The A354 can be seen above your head and you might hope for an underpass here but there is no such luck. The track veers right and you have to cross the main road to the Jubilee Trail sign opposite. Jubilee Trail actually goes through two copses ahead. We want to turn right for the path 150 metres along on the left. It hugs the woodland on the right. Follow this path as it turns right, still along the edge of woodland. Head for a large corrugated barn less than half a mile away. Go down past the barn to the farm track which leads to our lane.

Winterborne Whitchurch is less than half a mile away on the right.

Walk 29

Steeple – Tyneham

This walk can only be made when the Army Ranges are open. They are often open now, especially at holiday time. Check with Lulworth Cove Heritage Centre, Phone: 01929 400587. The army took over miles of beautiful coastland and the village of Tyneham was evacuated during the Second World War. Sadly the inhabitants have never been allowed to return to their homes which are now ruins. The church and village school have been restored and we are privileged to glimpse at the lessons and thoughts of yesterday's children. Ironically, the presence of the army has kept this area free of urban development and nature has benefitted. It is also free of pubs, shops and cafes, so bring your own refreshments.

Starting point: Steeple church. The road signposted 'To Steeple Church Only' curves behind the church. There is room here for three cars. GR912809

Maps: Outdoor Leisure 15 and Landranger 194, 195

Distance: 6 miles.

Terrain: Quite hilly

The Churches

St Michael and All Angels is in the little hamlet of Steeple, known as 'Stiple' in Domesday 1087. It has an idyllic setting, lying off the beaten track below the chalk ridge which crosses Purbeck. As you enter the road to the church, the manor is on the left and the church faces you across a spacious green. American visitors to this church must wonder why the ancestors of George Washington ever left England. The Lawrence family, who had intermarried with the Washingtons, once held the patronage of the manor. The Lawrence shield over the door of the north transept may have been the inspiration of the American flag's stars and stripes. The Perpendicular tower probably replaced an older Norman one. The stones below are small and the masonry rough. Above, the 16th-century stonework is more even. There is also Norman work in the lower part of the nave walls and in the round headed arches of the south doorway and the blocked north doorway. In the north wall is an early 13th-century lancet window. The transepts are 17th century. The south transept, now the vestry, houses an unusual barrel organ. The chancel was rebuilt by Nathaniel Bond, Prebendary 1852-1889. The Bond family held the manor from 1691.

Tyneham's church of St Mary is well maintained, although no villagers

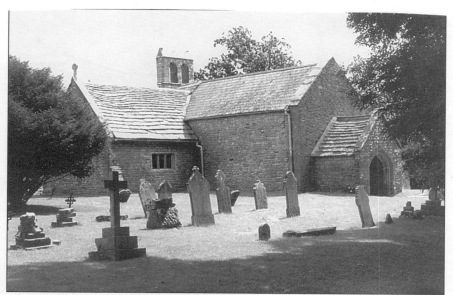

Tyneham church is in a deserted village amidst army ranges and can be visited
on open days

worship here. Visitors come to sample village life before 1943 when
Tyneham was evacuated to allow military training here. There has never
been more than a handful of grey stone cottages in the hamlet and now only
the church and school are left intact. The church is in the shape of a cross
with a piscina of AD 1300 in the north transept. The nave and north transept are in Early English and Decorated styles. The Gothic south transept
was built before 1852 by Rev. William Bond. The manor of Tyneham came
to the Bond family in 1683. There are monuments to Bond family servants,
Elizabeth Tarrant and Hannah Hunworth, nurse, a display of unusual gratitude. The early 20th-century east window of Madonna and Child has been
much admired. Outside, there are stone slates on much of the roof; the rest
has been tiled by the army. The greatest delight of Tyneham is the beautiful
countryside of hills and coast. Celtic, Roman and Saxon influence can be
seen all around.

The Walk

Keep strictly to marked paths when on the Army Ranges.

Go back towards, but not as far as, the 'Steeple Church' signpost and turn
left in 50 metres on a footpath through Manor Farm. Bear left across a field

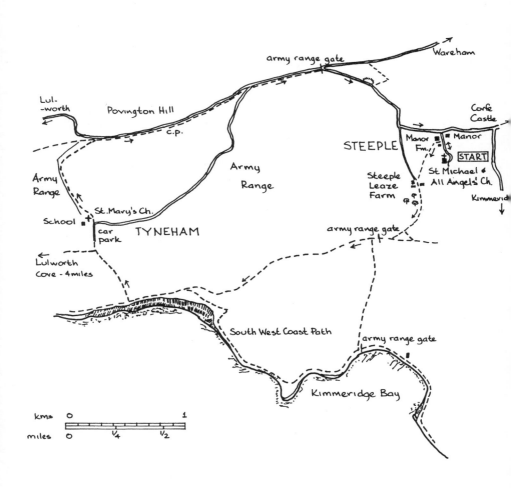

with earthworks and cross into the next field. Keep on route down to Steeple Leaze Farm. Veer left and go through the farmyard and across a stream into a small wood. Follow the stony path as it curves to the right and climbs up to the ridge above. Before you reach the top, you can look back down to Steeple in its sleepy rural setting. On the ridge, the scene changes to wide sweeps of unploughed land and hills above a wide shimmering sea. The entrance to the Army Ranges can be seen to the right. Follow the yellow markers and take the high route westward along the ridge. 'Lulworth' and 'Tyneham' are indicated. As you reach higher ground, the white cliffs of Lulworth Cove come into view. In about one mile you join the South West Coast Path, still heading west along the cliff. Now you can look across Worbarrow Tout, a raised headland, towards Portland. In 300 metres turn right following yellow markers down to Tyneham. Go through the wood, across the car park and into the village on the left.

After seeing the village of Tyneham, go behind the church and take the footpath climbing north to a higher ridge. This path follows a track with hard chippings. It curves right up to the highway along the ridge. A separate route is provided for walkers and we can walk beside the road unmolested by cars. We are heading east. In half a mile we pass the access road to Tyneham. There are magnificent views over the ranges to the sea. Another half a mile and the footpath ends. We come out onto the road and turn immediately right onto the lane back to Corfe. A chalk pit has been left open on the left as a typical example of stone extraction. In less than one mile we come to the turning marked 'To Steeple Church Only' and retrace our steps.

Walk 30

Worth Matravers – St Aldhelm's Chapel

This is a dramatic coastal walk between Norman churches. Much of it is along the top of a precipitous cliff. You need a fine day. This walk is not suitable for small children or for anyone without a good head for heights.

Starting point: Worth Matravers Car Park, outside the village on the Corfe Castle Road; GR973776

Maps: Outdoor Leisure 15 and Landranger 195

Distance: 5 miles or 7 miles

Terrain: along the top of steep cliffs and on rocky inland paths.

The Churches

St Nicholas is built of local Purbeck stone, as is the rest of the little village of Worth Matravers. It is on a hillside shelf near the coast and has always been a centre of stone quarrying. I passed a working quarry beside the track back from the coast. The truly Norman church was built in about 1100 of rubble with ashlar dressing. The early Norman tower arch, some Norman windows and the corbel which runs under the eaves are all original. The wonderful chancel arch with Norman zig zag mouldings and the south doorway have been brought from elsewhere and set into the church. The rare Tympanum above the south doorway shows the Virgin and two angels. These fine additions may have come from a monastery after the Dissolution. The Norman tower is in three stages with the smallest at the top. The pyramidal roof is Victorian.

St Aldhelm's Chapel stands square and rugged on the grassy top of the cliff at the southern tip of Purbeck. It is entirely Norman and entirely stone. The central pier and four rib vaults support the stone slated pyramidal roof. St Aldhelm, AD 640-709, may be the first English scholar and librarian. He wrote in Anglo-Saxon and Latin. In AD 705. he was appointed by his cousin, King Ine to be Bishop of Sherborne. The chapel may have been for the benefit of sailors. A beacon on top would have warned them off the rocks and a priest would have held mass for their safety.

The Walk

Head south down towards the village. Pass the duck pond on the left and post office and tea room on the right. The church can be seen ahead.

After visiting Worth Matravers church, resume your course, passing a play area on your right. At the edge of the village turn left and take the track marked 'Winspit'. Pass bungalows on your left and follow the track down as it veers left then right through a cleft in hills down to the sea, about a mile an a half in all. At the end on the right is an old quarry. From here stone was loaded directly onto barges in the sea below. We take the South West Coast Path going west from here. The path is behind the quarry and climbs the cliff above it. As you climb, turn to admire the view to Durlston Head. The cliff walk on a narrow path is about one and a half miles long and takes you to the southernmost part of Purbeck, St Aldhelm's Head. The last few metres is a climb up to St Aldhelm's Chapel, coastguard station and cottages.

It is possible to leave the walk here and follow the track past the coastguard cottages and away from the cliff. Worth Matravers can be seen ahead on the right. In one mile take the footpath on the right. Below in a fold of the

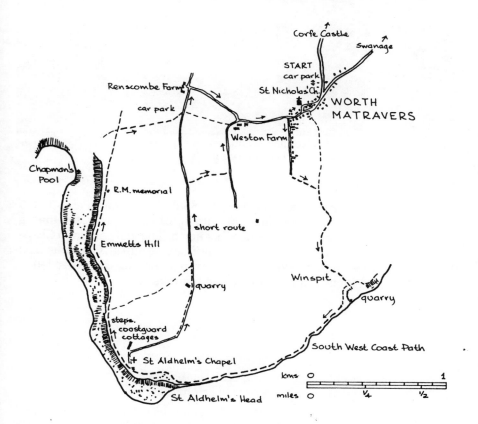

hills, facing the sea is a lone cottage with its own wind generator. You have a less idyllic view as you turn left and head for Weston Farm. Turn right for Worth Matravers.

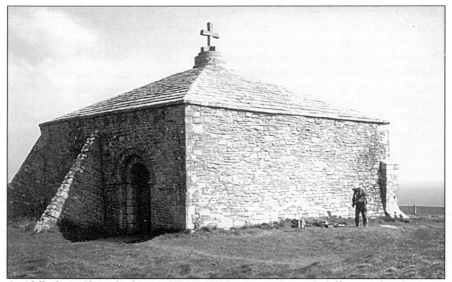

St Aldhelm's Chapel, also Norman, stands on an exposed cliff top. It has been a beacon for sailors

The Longer Walk

Continue around St Aldhelm's Head on the South West Coast Path. In 200 metres you have a long, steep descent with steps edged in stone, then a climb up to Emmetts Hill. You are heading north. The view down to Chapman's Pool and the coast beyond is outstandingly beautiful. Continue past the Royal Marines Memorial and take the first path on the right. Turn left at the car park and then turn right for Worth Matravers.

Upwey has a delightful Perpendicular church.
This is a popular village near Weymouth (Walk 31)

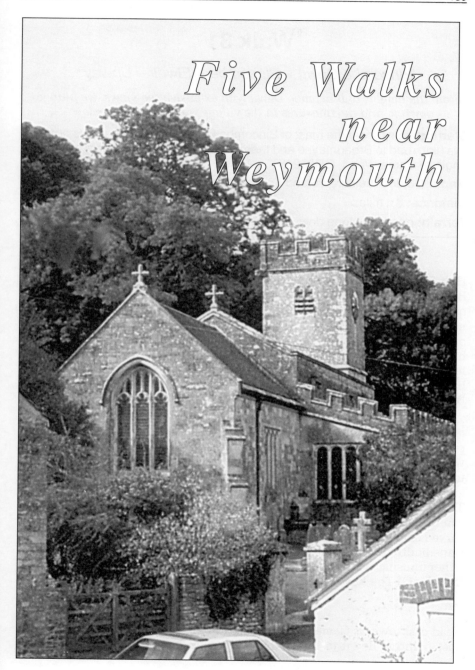

Five Walks near Weymouth

Walk 31

Bincombe Down – Bincombe – Elwell – Upwey

From the heights of Bincombe Down with extensive sea views, we plunge down to find the treasures in the villages near the coast below.

Starting point: near the mast of Bincombe Down. The golf course is next to this high road to Broadmayne and there is also parking further east at the triangle at Came Wood; GR682857.

Maps: Outdoor Leisure 15 and Landranger 194.

Distance: 6½ miles

Terrain: one long slope down and one up, otherwise, gently undulating.

The Churches

Holy Trinity is a simple little church in the peaceful, sequestered village of Bincombe, below downland. 'Beincombe' existed before the Norman Conquest. The present church is Early English in style with a Norman blocked north doorway. The font is Purbeck marble on a stone base. The windows on the south side are Perpendicular. The south door (1779) has a medieval holy water stoop next to it. The chancel was restored in 1862. Caius College, Cambridge has owned the church since 1570 and is still patron of the living. Late this century there has been and is a united Benefice of Bincombe, Broadway, Upwey and Buckland Ripers.

Upwey's Church of St Laurence is built of Upwey stone from the nearby local quarry. It is similar to Portland stone. The Upwey Wishing Well was a pre-Christian holy place. Christians may have found this an advantage when they built the first, probably wooden church. The present Perpendicular church was built between 1490 and 1520 and the porch roof with a gargoyle of a boy astride a wolf, water spout in its mouth is from this period. The north arcade in Ham Hill stone has one capital which harks back to pagan times. As you enter the church, turn right and meet the 'Green Man', carved on the last capital. He was an ancient emblem of fertility. The Victorians omitted him when they built the south arcade to match the north. Other unusual symbols are two Tudor roses, perhaps celebrating the end of the War Of The Roses in 1485. There is a fine Jacobean pulpit.

The Walk

Head east towards Came Wood. At a well-defined hedge, there is a finger post pointing down to Bincombe. Turn right here and follow the track down for over half a mile. At the tarmac road turn left for Bincombe and the church is ahead below.

From Bincombe church return to the village road and turn left. This is a no through road. In 200 metres the road crosses a stream and you turn right heading west across a field. Keep the hedge on your right and cross to the next field, which has horse stables. Go up above the stable to a corner of the field and continue west. Coombe Farm can be seen ahead. Pass the farm on your right, go under the railway bridge and emerge at suburban houses. At the corner with A354 stands a Catholic church. Cross the main road and turn right. Walk along the pavement, passing a pub on the right. Turn left at a finger post and go down a lane with little cottages on the left. At the next finger post you have a choice; take the most acute turning to the right. Cross a small field to another row of handsome cottages. Turn right and cross over to Little Hill. Do not be tempted up here. Instead, go up the track to a pretty little detached cottage and turn left, going behind the row of hand-

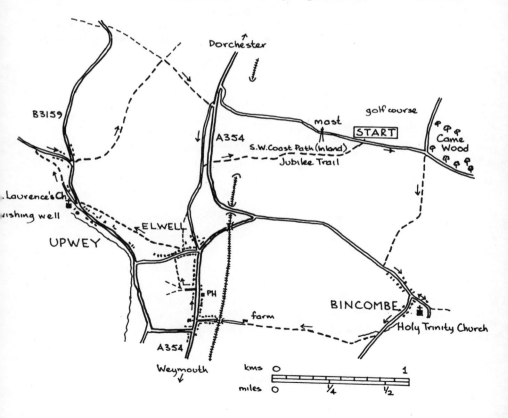

some cottages. This is Jubilee Trail, which you follow north-west with a hill on the right and fine trees on the slope over to the left. Soon the path is restricted to an alleyway past houses and then emerges at B3159 opposite the lovely Upwey church. Go down to the Wishing Well tea rooms and restaurant on the left and Church Lane is on the right.

From Upwey church continue along the lane which narrows then becomes a grassy path. In less than half a mile you reach a tarmac lane and turn right to go back to to B3159. Cross to the bridleway opposite. This curves to the right and then follows the valley gently uphill to its head. In over half a mile at the top left-hand corner of the field, you come to crosspaths. The Inland Coast Path follows the ridge. Turn right here and you have fine views over Weymouth and Portland on the right. In 300 metres just before A354, turn right down a track which runs parallel with the main road. In 300 metres look for a hidden style and turn left. The Jubilee Trail joins the Coast Path here. With great care, cross A354 to the track opposite that takes you past the mast on Bincombe Hill, past tumuli. Myth has it that sweet music can be heard emanating from one of the round barrows at midday for anyone who puts an ear to the top. If you resist this and keep on course, you arrive back at the starting point near the golf course.

Walk 32

Holworth – Chaldon Down – Durdle Door – Winfrith Newburgh (Owermoigne is an optional extra)

From a quiet lane we head for the spectacular Dorset Coast and walk over downland to the famous Durdle Door, a natural rock archway in the sea. This route has steep inclines and is slippery when wet so an alternative inland route is included. We return from Winfrith via the five Marys in remote downland.

Starting point: the verge on the road to Holworth south of Owermoigne; GR766841.

Maps: Outdoor Leisure 15 and Landranger 194

Distance: Approximately 12 miles (6 or 7 miles with buses).

Public transport: Bus 103 will take you from Lulworth Cove 2.30 and 6.30pm calling at Winfrith Newburgh Church 2.42 and 6.42pm then on to Owermoigne. Monday to Saturday at the time of writing (First Dorset Transit 01305 262992).

Terrain: hilly in places

The Churches

St Christopher stands peacefully among trees at the western end of the pretty village of Winfrith Newburgh. The Hundred of Winfrith is mentioned in Domesday. The little Winfrith stream flows alongside the church. A handsome Victorian lych gate leads to a Norman-style entrance with chevron mouldings. The chancel arch is 13th century and the Perpendicular tower has gargoyles from the battlements.

St Nicholas, Chaldon Herring, is delightfully situated in a sweep of downland. The original Norman building has been lost in 15th century and Victorian restorations. The Perpendicular tower remains unspoilt. A local craftsman, Canon Gildea made the pulpit, lectern and altar table.

Owermoigne's Church of St Michael was restored in 1883 yet retains an aura of its distant past. There was a Saxon settlement at 'Ogre' and John Le Moigne was the patron. 'Ogre' changed to 'Oweres' and the two combined to Owermoigne. Moigne Court to the north is a renowned 13th-century court house. An heiress of the Moignes married a Stourton and one of their descendants murdered his guests at dinner. Queen Mary is said to have ordered the murderer, Lord Stourton to be hanged with a silken rope, silk because he was noble. In the church, only an Early English window in the

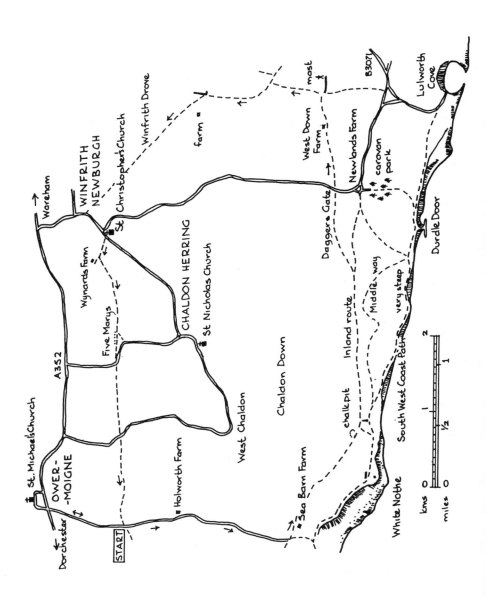

tower has the antiquity of Moigne Court. The tower and chancel are Perpendicular.

The Walk

Head south along the lane and through Holworth Farm. At the division of 'Private Roads', follow the road on the right heading for the coast, a mile away. A view over Weymouth Harbour opens on the right. The thatched Sea Barn Farm is on the left. Turn left here towards Lulworth and walk east with the fence on the left. This downland route runs parallel with the more arduous South West Coast Path and still offers views over the sea. **Warning:** both routes are slippery in wet weather. The shortest, safest route is on the left and well-marked to Daggers Gate, two miles away.

If you wish to see Durdle Door, turn acutely right after a chalk pit on the left and go down towards the sea. At the South West Coast Path turn left and head for a small obelisk. After passing the obelisk, decide whether you want to take the roller coaster path close to the sea on the right or the left-hand gentler way. This passes Countryside Commission stiles on the left and it is still possible to escape to the inland Daggers Gate path if need be. Otherwise, follow the downland curves of the middle way. After the second curve, find a stile on the left (not a Countryside Commission stile) and cross into the next piece of downland with the arch of Durdle Door in the sea below. Go gently down to the bay. Continue along the Coastal Path to reach the steps down to Durdle Door and the beach.

From Durdle Door you can keep on the coastal path for over half a mile to Lulworth Cove and catch the bus back to Owermoigne.

I propose to turn inland through a caravan site where refreshments can be had. Continue north through Newlands Farm and up to a public road. Turn left and the bridleway of Daggers Gate is 100 metres away.

Turn right here up to West Down Farm. Ignore the permissive bridleway to the left just past the farm and head for the mast. At crossways just before the mast, turn left and go for half a mile heading north over downland with the hedge on your right. At crosspaths there is a double hedge facing you. Enter and turn left to walk between the hedges for half a mile. You emerge at a cross track where a farmhouse can be seen below on the left. Cross diagonally left into another enclosed path. This opens onto a wide, straight farm track, Winfrith Drove all the way down to the village. The old nuclear power station can be seen away to the right. When you reach Winfrith Newburgh, a quiet pretty place in contrast with its once formidable neighbour, turn left for the church.

From Winfrith Newburgh church continue on the lane west towards Chaldon Herring, passing the church and a nursing home on the left. In 50 metres turn right towards Wynards Farm. The five Marys are indicated. In

100 metres fork left towards the five Marys. These are tumuli half a mile away. Our path heads east on a downland ridge for over two miles with fine views all around. Chaldon Down is ahead on the left. After the five Marys you come to a tarmac road and can make a detour down to Chaldon Herring below on the left.

From the five Marys continue west and cross the tarmac road. The way is indicated to White Horse. We do not go as far as this. In half a mile cross the West Chaldon road and keep to our easterly route across fields. The path sinks then rises to the start of the walk on Holworth Road. Here another detour can be made to Owermoigne church, less than one mile away to the north.

Owermoigne church is among houses in the village
just north of the A352

Walk 33
East Lulworth – Wool – Coombe Keynes

From the splendour of 17th-century Lulworth Castle, you walk through the park on permissive paths, then on public bridleways over heathland and woods to the edge of the busy town of Wool. Return through the pretty Dorset village of Coombe Keynes. There are four churches of individual character to visit on this walk.

Starting point: Lulworth Castle Car Park. The castle opens at 10 am (not Saturday, Christmas Eve or Christmas Day). You can park before opening times. GR856822

Maps: Outdoor Leisure 15 and Landranger 194

Distance: 8 miles

Local Information: Coombe Heath is next to the army ranges. Red flags indicate the edge of the range.

Public Transport: First Dorset Transit (Tel: 01305 262992) Monday to Saturday provides a 'hail and ride' service between East Lulworth and Wool, calling at Shaggs and Coombe Keynes – useful if you wish to shorten the walk. At the time of writing Bus 103 runs as follows: Depart East Lulworth: 9.32 am, 12.32 pm, 3.32 pm; Depart Wool Station: 11.10 am, 2.10 pm, 6.10 pm. There is also a Dorset Linkrider (Tel: 01929 553528).

Terrain: Gently undulating

The Churches

St Andrew's, East Lulworth, is built of Purbeck stone and carstone. The church was the centre of the parish until the end of 18th century when the village houses were moved outside the park walls.

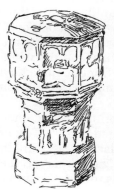

Only the handsome 15th-century church tower remains from those days. Thomas Hardy, who assisted John Hicks in rebuilding the rest of the church in 1862, wrote 'This tower is one of exceptional grace and artistic proportions in curious contrast to the customary local architecture of so late a date'. Inside, the tower arch and font are also 15th century. Nearby stands Lulworth Castle, a square impressive building with Purbeck ashlar at the east front and coursed rubble on the other sides. Built 1608 -1610 as a private country residence, the Roman Catholic Weld family has owned the castle since 1641.

East Lulworth Roman Catholic church, in the castle grounds is a fine, domed building

St Mary's stands on the other side of the castle. It was the first Roman Catholic church to be built in England since the Reformation under Henry VIII. In 1792, King George III gave Thomas Weld permission to build a Catholic chapel, provided it did not look like a church. Italian builders created a domed building with Tuscan porch and columns. 'A Pantheon in miniature', according to Fanny Burney. Inside, white Purbeck columns support three galleries and an altar space. The dome is painted blue and white for sky and clouds. It is an unusual and beautiful church.

At Wool, Holy Rood is a solid Victorian church with a stout 15th-century tower built of grey ashlar. It is hard to believe that, until recently, this was the parochial chapel to tiny Combe Keynes. In 1384, there was a Wool Chapel which was rebuilt in 1865 and lengthened by 12 feet. The north arcade is 14th century, the triple chancel arch is 14th century and the windows mainly 15th century. Those in the north wall come from Coombe Keynes. There are two fonts; the Wool font is 15th century and the Coombe font in the south-east corner is 13th century.

North of Wool, across the River Frome, is Woolbridge Manor, once the home of the locally powerful Turbervilles who inspired Hardy's 'Tess of the d'Urbervilles'. The open coffin where Angel Clare placed Tess is still in the grounds of Bindon Abbey, an ancient Cistercian religious house, ruined at the Dissolution. The Turbervilles rest in the churchyard of Wool church.

In Coombe Keynes, Holy Rood, built of flint and stone, was made redundant in 1974. Once the centre of a large medieval village, it is now the last building south in a much reduced hamlet. The manor of 'Cume', mentioned in Domesday, was held by the Keynes family for 200 years, hence the name 'Combe Keynes'. The family lived at Tarrant Keyneston and they died out in 14th century. In 1641 Humphrey Weld bought the estate. In mid-19th century Nathaniel Bond, rector of Steeple and Tyneham managed to persuade the Roman Catholic Joseph Weld to make a major contribution to the restoration of the church which had become dilapidated. The work was carried out by John Hicks, no doubt assisted by Thomas Hardy who made a fine drawing of the font. Sadly by 1970 there were fewer people in the village and the church was closed. With the help of Sir Joseph Weld, grandson of the above benefactor, the villagers have bought back the church and it is again part of village life. The chancel arch, transferred by Hicks from the old arcade and the tower are Early English. A silver chalice from this church is on display at Victoria and Albert Museum.

The Walk

This walk starts on permissive paths through the grounds of the castle. A 'paths' ticket', currently costing £2, can be had from reception. A full ticket will allow you to see inside the castle and the Catholic chapel. *If you cannot obtain a 'walks ticket', it is possible to start walking along the fairly quiet road towards Wool for one mile with the park wall on your left and turn right at the first bridleway at the hamlet of Shaggs. (Or take the bus 103). Then pick up the walk at the second paragraph below, marked *.*

Before starting the walk, you can visit the nearby parish church with lofty tower. From here, return towards the car park then head for the clearly marked entrance. Follow the prescribed route to the castle. Here the paths are indicated with a finger post. Follow the route of Path 2 which heads north towards the edge of woodland, passing the Catholic chapel on the left. After the wooded rise, the path curves right and down to Park Lodge Farm half a mile from the castle. Turn right here and go along the access lane to the farm. It leads to the hamlet of Shaggs on the Lulworth to Wool road. Cross the road to the public bridleway opposite.

By whichever way you arrived here, walk along the bridleway, a farm track. The track curves right and gently rises along the edge of woodland. One of the permissive paths also follows this route for half a mile, then descends to the lake on the left. The public way bears right into the wood then immediately left to follow the farmtrack between hedgerows. The track heads north-east and becomes a grassy way beside a copse on the right. Keep on course as far as the Army Ranges where you should find a red flag flying. Turn left here and follow the bridleway beside the range heading north-west. Cross through the thin woodland into Coombe Heath with heather, gorse and other sand-loving plants. This is a nature reserve next to the Army Ranges on the right. In 250 metres veer left and strike out across the heath. The path is well defined and woodland can be seen ahead.

You enter the wood near Oak Tree Farm on the right. Do not turn left but keep straight on along the track through mainly deciduous trees. In 250 metres at crosspaths go straight on towards Woodstreet. This path veers left out of the wood. It then continues along the edge of the wood that is on your right. In less than half a mile you reach a track down to Woodstreet Farm. Do not go down to the farm. Instead, turn left on the footpath up a field to a tarmac lane. Turn left and walk along the lane for 50 metres. Just after the Forestry Commission entrance to Cole Wood on the right, turn right at a footpath signposted to Wool church. The path is well used and heads north-west to a gap in the hedge. Go through, turn right and hug the hedge on the right for 75 metres. Go through another gap at the field corner and Wool church can be seen ahead. At a junction with the village track, turn left for the church. *Bindon Abbey is indicated to the right. A visit to these remains, in private grounds and only viewed from the road, would add half a mile.*

After visiting Wool church, opposite a thatcher's cottage, continue along Church Lane. You come to a green with pretty cottages and a stream with ducks. *(Shops, a pub and tea room near the station are to the right).* Turn left after the stream and left again at the B3071 and walk along the road for 350 metres, passing a road on the right, the school, then bungalows on the left. Turn right into a hedge-lined track signposted to New Buildings. These are no more than a large barn over half a mile away. Turn left at the barn and go along the tarmac lane back up to the B3071. Turn right and walk along the verge of the main road for 200 metres. Turn left to the little thatched village of Coombe Keynes. The church is up a track on the right, next to the last cottage. You may apply for the key at a cottage near the entrance to the track.

From Coombe Keynes church, return to the village and turn right.* After 250 metres along the Lulworth road, turn right into a track between hedges with a little detached house on the right. You are now on one of the permissive bridleways. Continue up past a copse on the left. After this Hardy Way crosses the track. You pass an enclosure with electrical equipment on the right. The deserted gate house at the edge of the Lulworth estate can be seen ahead. Turn left here then cross into the Castle grounds. Follow the arrows and go down back to Park Lodge Farm. From here, retrace your steps to the castle.

Note: if you do not have a paths ticket, continue along the road to Lulworth, turn right at B3070 and right again to the castle car park.

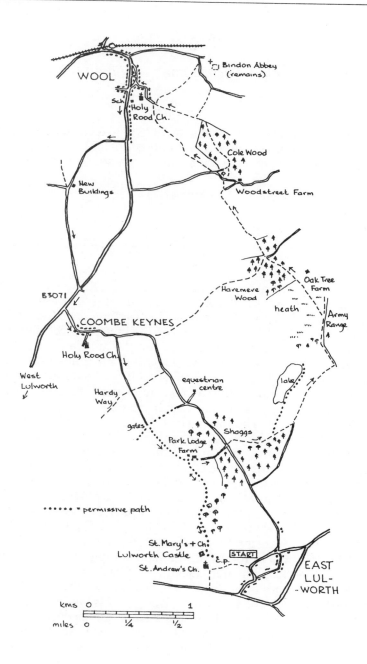

WOOL

Bindon Abbey (remains)

Sch.

Holy Rood Ch.

Cole Wood

New Buildings

Woodstreet Farm

Oak Tree Farm

Havemere Wood

heath

Army Range

B3071

COOMBE KEYNES

Holy Rood Ch.

West Lulworth

Hardy Way

equestrian centre

lake

gates

Park Lodge Farm

Shaggs

•••••• = permissive path

St. Mary's + Ch.
Lulworth Castle
St. Andrew's Ch.

START

E.P.

EAST LUL- -WORTH

kms 0 _____ 1

miles 0 ¼ ½

Walk 34

West Knighton – Whitcombe – Winterborne Came

This is a pleasant rural walk with the added reward of three medieval churches.

Starting point: West Knighton church GR733876 (Limited parking. Alternatively, drive towards Whitcombe and turn left before reaching the village. Park on grass verges near crosspaths, marked on the sketch map, GR712873.)

Maps: Outdoor Leisure 15, Landranger 194

Distance: 5½ miles

Terrain: Gently undulating

The Churches

St Peter's is still central to village life in West Knighton. Over 1000 years of Christianity are represented in a Norman chancel arch and an east window over the altar. In Domesday the name 'Chenistetone' from the Anglo-Saxon 'cnihtatun' meant a place of lower nobles and knights. Most of the church is 13th century with Transitional columns in the arcade and Early English windows in the transept. The tower is built of random small stone in the 13th century lower two stages and ashlar at the 16th-century top.

Whitcombe church, in the loving care of the Churches Conservation Trust, is a stone memorial to ages past. It is a single cell with Saxon stones included in the Norman building. The 12th-century nave has wall paintings on either side of the blocked Norman door. St Christopher was painted about 1400. He carries the Christ Child on his shoulder as he wades through a river towards a leafy bank. The chancel has a triple lancet window. Other windows are Perpendicular. The tower is 16th century. The church was linked to Milton Abbey before the Dissolution and has no known dedication. After the Dissolution it passed to the Tregonwells and then to the Damers who still live at Came House. The Dorset dialect poet, William Barnes was rector here and referred to his clerk as 'Archbishop of York'. His clerk was in the habit of remonstrating: 'Now you have got to mind I; I be the second man in the church, I be'.

St Peter's, Winterborne Came, is tucked away behind high walls and trees, next to the Palladian Came House. This mainly Perpendicular church is built of grey ashlar. Inside is an ornate Jacobean pulpit where William Barnes preached for over 20 years. He walked from the thatched rectory on the main road to his churches and to see his parishioners. He

Whitcombe is a hamlet of thatched cottages with a little gem of a church

was a phenomenal linguist with some knowledge of 65 languages. He died in 1886 and is buried in the churchyard. The church also has an impressive 17th-century altar tomb with alabaster effigies of John Meller and his wife. The rood screen is 16th century.

The Walk

From West Knighton church, follow the neighbouring wall capped with tiles in Dorset style. At the road junction turn right along Jubilee Trail. Go down through rough ground and keep straight on at crosspaths. At the next crosspaths, turn left following Jubilee Trail due west. In half a mile it crosses to the left of the hedgerow. A farm track intercepts and goes up to the main road on the left. Cross the track and bear right by the edge of the thatched village of Whitcombe. Go through stables and then the paddock behind. In the left-hand far corner of the paddock, Jubilee Trail struggles through enclosing hedges and turns left to the main A352. Turn left here and follow the verge for 50 metres before turning into the haven of this delightful church.

From Whitcombe church, cross A352 diagonally left to the finger post pointing west to Winterborne Came. This is still Jubilee Trail. Follow it up to woodland. Go through Cole Hill Wood and veer slightly right and down through an open field with Came Park on the right. Go down to a pair of cot-

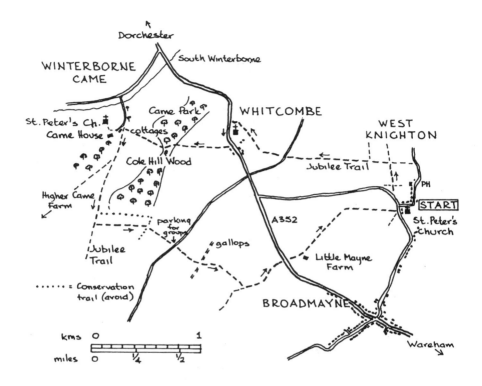

tages where Jubilee Trail turns left. Here you leave the trail to visit the church but note the way for the return trek. Behind the cottages are trees which separate Winterborne Came from the rest of the world. Go through the trees to the tarmac drive, a high wall and a few cottages. Turn left along the drive and, just before Came House, turn right to the church.

From Winterborne Came church return to the pair of cottage beyond the trees and continue your pursuit of Jubilee Trail by turning right and heading south on a well defined chalk track, slippery when wet. In less than half a mile the path forks. Do not take the right-hand track to Higher Came Farm. Keep to Jubilee Trail to the left uphill. Ignore the new Conservation Route to the wood on the left. Continue another 50 metres and turn left onto the bridleway. Here you finally leave Jubilee Trail. The bridleway heads east across a cultivated field with the hedge on the left. At the field boundary you cross the Conservation Route again. Follow the public bridleway through the hedge into the next field and down to a tarmac lane.

This is the Starting Point for large groups (see sketch map). If you fall into this category, start here, continue to the end of the next paragraph and loop back to the beginning of the walk instructions. Everybody else, just complete this final paragraph:

Cross the lane to the track opposite. This goes up to woodland, which you pass on your right. Cross the gallops and follow the track to a T-junction. Turn left here and north-east., keeping the hedge on your right. The path narrows and is enclosed by hedges just before the A352 which you can hear ahead. Cross this busy road with care to the footpath opposite. Make for the farmhouse, Little Mayne Farm and pass it on your right. Then cross the next field diagonally to the right-hand corner. Negotiate the Olympian stile and continue north-west, still on cultivated land. At the farm track which crosses our path, climb to the far side of the hedge and turn right. West Knighton church can be seen ahead.

Walk 35

Langton Herring – East Fleet – Chickerell Hill – Corton

From a quiet Dorset village we walk along banks of the unique Chesil Beach to a smugglers' hideout at Fleet village. Fleet is also the name of the lagoon formed 80,000 years ago. Next we climb to the tiny hamlet of Corton in downland. We take in four churches, each with a distinctive charm of its own. This walk can be done in three parts; Part 2 is the whole walk, Part 1 includes Chesil Beach, Part 3 includes the lovely ancient church of Corton.

Starting point: Elm Tree Pub, Langton Herring. Parking is provided for ramblers who buy drinks. GR615824

Maps: Outdoor Leisure 15 and Landranger 194

Distances: Part 1, Langton Herring to Fleet 6½ miles; Part 2, Langton Herring to Fleet – Chickerell Hill – Corton 12 miles; Part 3, Langton Herring to Corton 7 miles

Terrain: varied, some hills, not too strenuous.

The Churches

St Peter's, Langton Herring, was rebuilt by the early Victorians. Only the tower and some lancet windows survive from the old, probably 13th-century church. Langetone was the Anglo-Saxon name for the village and there would have been a church here then. The name 'Herring' comes from the 'Harang' family who held the manor and fortified it in 1337. Their manor house has gone now! Some of the field boundaries here have stone walls from local pits. Langton Cross, hewn from one large stone, stands east of the village and is believed to have been valued by pilgrims to Abbotsbury. Part 1 of our walk goes past Langton Cross.

East Fleet's Old Church is built entirely of local Forest Marble. Only the chancel remains from the old church when a storm in 1824 destroyed the rest of the building and also many cottages. The name 'Fleet' comes from the Anglo-Saxon 'Floet' meaning a tidal inlet. There was a church here in Norman times with a priest called Bollo. The Mohuns came by Fleet in 1566. Their name will be forever linked with the village, thanks to the smuggling novel by Meade Faulkner, 'Moonfleet'. The vault of this chancel is vividly described as a hiding place for wines and spirits. There is said to be a secret passage to The Fleet from here.

In Fleet, we visit Holy Trinity. In 1829 John Gould, the vicar paid for a handsome new church set in woodland. It has a fine decorated chancel

Corton is a little Early English chapel, perfect in its simplicity

ceiling and a low-pitched nave ceiling in 18th-century Gothic style. There is a monument to the vicar's son, also John Gould.

How ironic that Corton, a tiny hamlet with a grey stone farm and chapel of St Bartholomew, otherwise remote from the 20th century, should be so plagued by electric pylons and cables. In Domesday it was called 'Corfeton', meaning the town of the gap. The manor and chapel passed from the hands of De Curcelle to the Courtneys and thence to the famous Mohuns. They lost it in the Civil War. The chapel was also lost then and used as a farm building. Fortunately, the chapel was overlooked at the Reformation and has kept its ancient stone altar. This simple, single cell, Early English chapel was rescued from its fate as a hen house and stable by Mr James Crane. We are fortunate to see it restored to its ancient beauty.

The Walk

Parts 1 and 2

From the Elm Tree Pub, head for the nearby church. Go along the lane, which passes the church and curves down around it. At a T-junction, follow the lane to the left and in 100 metres turn left onto a track. In 50 metres, this bends to the right down to Chesil Beach and the sea. Ahead is a row of windswept cottages. Turn left at the Coast Path, also marked 'Hardy Way'.

The water of the Fleet is alive with wild birds. In less than one mile the path goes below the massive buildings of Moonfleet Manor Hotel. The old part, dating back to 17th century, was once the home of the Mohuns. After the hotel you come to a wide grassy way above the Fleet to the right and with sloping pasture to the left. After a fine, dry-stone wall, you reach the bay at East Fleet. Turn inland here to the chancel of the village church, damaged when the sea invaded East Fleet in 1824. The chancel is on the left, just before the cottages of Butter Street.

After visiting East Fleet, go along Butter Street to Fleet Road and turn left. The 'new' church of 1829, Holy Trinity as was the old church, is 300 metres away.

From Holy Trinity, Fleet, continue along Fleet Road for 100 metres and turn right after the last cottage. Here is a mown grass path down to the hedge. Go to the right-hand corner, cross a footbridge over a stream and after a stile, turn immediately left to the next corner, keeping the hedge on your left. Go through to the next field, which you cross and turn right with the hedge on your right. Go up to B3157 at Chickerell Hill. Turn right and walk along the road for 50 metres. Cross to the footpath opposite and head north. Hug the hedge on the left. In 250 metres go left through the hedge canopy and turn right to cross to a corner of the field. Veer left and head north. Do not be tempted along Barr Lane, a rough track to the right. Instead, find the way north up through rough ground and through a small new plantation. Keep straight on towards a little fenced pond. Keep to the left of this and the path is accompanied by a little stream. As you approach pylons turn right and cut a left corner off the next field then resume your northerly course. Go past a barn on the right and the view ahead opens to woodland and fields. Go down to the fine, new, four-fingered post at the edge of the wood, Broad Coppice.

Part 1: Langton Cross is marked to the left and offers the most direct way back to Langton Herring. Keep heading west across field for one mile, passing Tatton Farm away to the right. When you reach B3157, turn left and walk beside the road for 100 metres. The turning to Langton Herring is to the right and Langton Cross is on the corner here.

Part 2: (the complete walk) From the new, four-fingered post, enter the edge of Broad Coppice following the 'Tatton' direction. Cross a plank over a stream and you soon emerge from the wood. Once outside the wood, turn left following the edge of the wood. Head north-east across a long field with the wood on your left. At a row of poplar trees turn right up to Nottington Lane. Turn left and walk along the lane for 250 metres. Pass Tatton Farm and Tatton House on the left. Turn right into a field and head downhill keeping hedges on your right

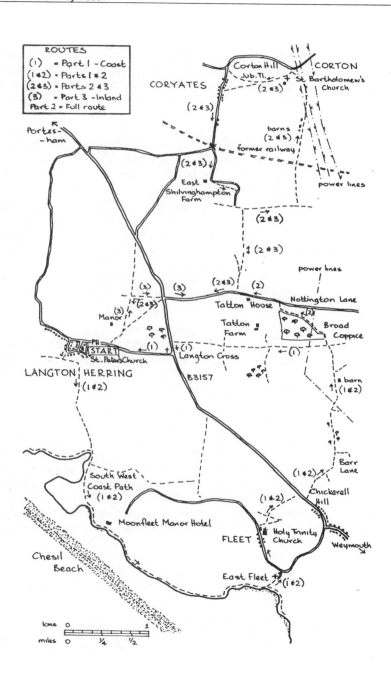

ROUTES
(1) = Part 1 - Coast
(1&2) = Parts 1 & 2
(2&3) = Parts 2 & 3
(3) = Part 3 - Inland
Part 2 = Full route

Part 3 and Part 2 follow the same route here:

A single plank takes you across the stream into the next field. Go gently uphill on a farm track. In 250 metres at a T-junction, turn right and cross two fields, the first short and the second long. You are walking along the brow of a hill. From the second field the tiny, light grey hamlet of Corton can be seen away to the left. The mass of pylons forms a grotesque background to this otherwise idyllic place. Look out for the farm track on the left which will take you to Corton. A ruined dairy, just one wall, is at the start of the track. This leads down to cross the dismantled railway and then starts climbing. Go past an assortment of barns on your left then climb up to Corton, passing under pylon cables on your way.

From Corton church head west through the churchyard gate onto downland. This is Jubilee Trail and curves round Corton Hill. There is a path off to the left to Coryates but it is easier to stay on Jubilee Trail as far as crossroads then turn left. Go down the lane through the hamlet of Coryates to the railway bridge and turn left. The footpath follows a track to East Shilvinghampton Farm. Turn left at the farm, cross a field and join the farm track south. This should be familiar territory and you retrace your steps to Tatton House.

At Nottington Lane turn right and in half a mile cross B3157 to bridleways diagonally opposite. Follow the right-hand fork for 250 metres to crosspaths. Turn left and cross a field to the wall at the bottom. Continue south-west through the manor house grounds of Langton Herring. At the tarmac lane turn right then first left back to the car park and a drink.

Part 3: Start at Langton Herring pub and turn left away from the church. At T-junction turn right towards Langton Cross. We do not go as far as the cross. In 150 metres on the left an animal sanctuary is marked. Take the second entrance and pass the manor house on your left. When you emerge from the manor/sanctuary grounds, go straight on heading north over the middle of the field and up to the hedge. Turn right just before the hedge and in 250 metres you reach B3157. Cross to the road opposite and walk for half a mile until you come to a footpath on the left down into a field with a hedge on the right. Continue as for joint Part 3 and Part 2 walk above *(See text in italics).*

The Minster's twin towers are quite distinctive. Wimborne Minster is justly proud of this large church dating from Norman times. (Walk 36)

Five Walks near Wimborne Minster

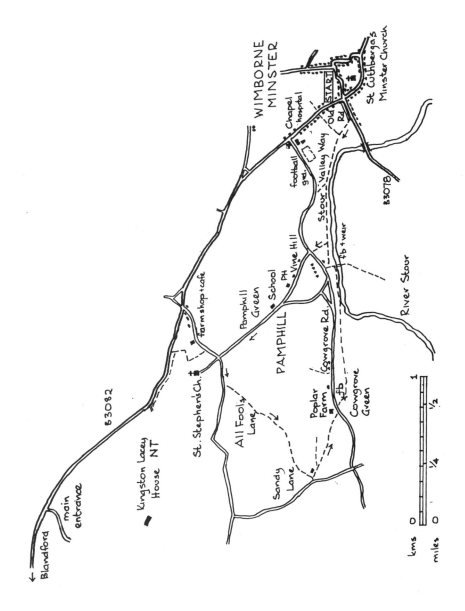

Walk 36

Wimborne Minster – Kingston Lacy
– St Margaret's Leper Chapel

This is mainly a town and riverside walk with an opportunity to visit a magnificent 17ᵗʰ-century country house, cared for by National Trust.

Starting point: Parking 'Pay and Display' on the western edge of Wimborne Minster, opposite 'Pudding and Pye' and 'The Green Man' pubs. GR006000

Maps: Explorer 118 and Landranger 195

Distance: about 5 miles

Terrain: Mainly flat, one hill.

The Churches

St Cuthberga dominates the busy market town of Wimborne Minster. The two towers, of similar height, are unique. The older, 12ᵗʰ-century, central tower once had a spire which collapsed in 1600, hurting no-one but damaging the quire. High on the outside of the 15ᵗʰ-century west tower is the Quarter Jack, a figure of a grenadier who strikes the quarter hour. Also distinctive are the mottled brown and grey heathstones on the outside. Inside, the Norman arches of the central crossing and the Transition-Norman arches of the nave are most impressive. The entrances from the transepts to the aisles have 13ᵗʰ-century Purbeck shafts. The late Norman font of Purbeck marble had all decoration removed by the Puritans. Earlier vandals have also made an impact: in the 11ᵗʰ century, Danes destroyed the nunnery, which had been founded by Cuthberga in AD 705. A college for secular canons replaced the nunnery in 1043. This in turn was demolished at the Dissolution. Fortunately the Minster survived and we can enjoy its treasures, which include a 14ᵗʰ-century astronomical clock.

St Margaret's and St Anthony's Chapel was built in 13ᵗʰ century to serve the nearby leper hospital.

St Stephen's, Kingston Lacy, has a colourful combination of stones: Studland sandstone and Purbeck stone. The present church, built in 1907 in late Decorated style, is light and airy and stands at the end of a long avenue of oaks in parkland. The site of the 11ᵗʰ-century church is unknown.

The Walk

Walk away from town along Old Road. The road turns right and you follow the footpath, signed to 'Eyebridge'. This path is part of the Stour Valley Way and initially passes through allotments then through fields beside the River

Stour. When a weir comes into view, look out for a footpath signposted 'Pamphill' on the right. Turn right onto this path across a field to a stile at a T-junction of roads. Walk up the road, Vine Hill, opposite. The road climbs steeply passing a pub just short of the top of the hill. Continue straight along the road, passing the village school on the right, to reach Kingston Lacy church in about half a mile.

If you wish to visit Kingston Lacy House and Gardens, return to main church gates and turn left, then left again along a footpath into the woods. The path leads to the B3082. You do not need to go as far as the main road; a new path, Harry's Walk leads to the pedestrian entrance to the House and Gardens.

To return to Wimborne, from the church gates turn right to walk along Abbott Street. In about 200 metres turn left into a track just before the notice '542 Abbey Street'. This hedge-lined, pebbly track is All Fools Lane. It goes steadily downhill for half a mile. At a grassy space at the bottom there are several beguiling finger posts. Turn immediately left following the 'Bridleway' sign and pass the little brick cottage on the left. A wide spacious route leads you to the Cowgrove Green. A pond is on your right and Poplar Farm on the left.

Here you have a choice of ways:

1. Bear left onto Cowgrove Road and follow the road for about one and a half miles to the Leper Chapel of St Margaret. Turn right and walk down the B3082 to the start of this walk.

2. From Poplar Farm cross to the cottage opposite and walk along the edge of the Green with a hedge on your left. Cross the footbridge and look for the path in the corner on the left. This is a well-defined path, not shown on O.S maps, back to the River Stour where kingfishers might be spotted. The twin towers of Wimborne Minster come into view. Follow the river as far as the football ground where you can turn left up to Cowgrove Road and continue as direction 1 above or cut this out and return through the allotments to the car park.

The Minster and Town Centre are well worth a visit and just a short walk away.

Walk 37

(White Mill, Sturminster Marshall) – Shapwick – Crawford Bridge – Tarrant Crawford – Tarrant Keyneston – Shapwick (– Sturminster Marshall).

This figure-of-eight walk follows the course of the Rivers Stour and Tarrant to visit the interesting churches which have grown up on the banks. A visit to Tarrant Crawford in February is rewarded with banks of snowdrops and yellow winter aconites.

Starting point: National Trust Car Park near White Mill outside Sturminster Marshall beyond the ancient bridge over the River Stour. GR958007. The Shorter Walk, marked *, starts and finishes at Shapwick GR937017

Maps: Explorer 118 and Landranger 195

Distance: Longer walk: 10 miles; shorter walk: 6 miles

Terrain: Fairly flat

The Churches

The church of St Mary in Sturminster Marshall has brown and grey stones. William Marshall, who gave his name to the village, also signed Magna Carta, the first signature after that of King John. The church retains some vestiges of the 12th century in the north arcade's round arches. The arch from the chancel to the north chapel is 13th century. The length of the church is accentuated by having no arch between nave and chancel. It is a large church, restored by the Victorians.

From its favoured position on the banks of the River Stour, St Bartholomew's in Shapwick has seen many changes. Romans passing by on their way to Dorchester forded the river near here. This church has a Norman north doorway and a 12th-century bay in the north arcade. The north chapel is Perpendicular and the chancel Victorian. The nave and tower are Decorated. Here again the stone is mixed; chequered flint and stone make up the main pattern.

Stone and flint are the materials of this solitary St Mary's in Tarrant Crawford. There is a sense of loneliness here. Yet this is the birthplace of Bishop Poore who founded Salisbury Cathedral and returned to be buried here. Tarrant Crawford had the largest nunnery in the country. The nuns had a window overlooking the altar. The nunnery was completely destroyed at the Dissolution and there are few traces of the vast building. The church is mainly 12th century with a priest's door of that period in the chancel. The windows, apart from the three-light one near the pulpit and two

Sturminster Marshall has a large church near the River Stour

one-light ones at the west end, are 13ᵗʰ century. There are 13ᵗʰ-and 14ᵗʰ-century wall paintings. The 14ᵗʰ-century painting in the nave depicts scenes in the life of St Margaret of Antioch, including her martyrdom. This colourful past has vanished. All now is peaceful. Only the occasional tractor passes along the lane to the nearby Georgian farmhouse. The church is in the care of the Churches Conservation Trust.

All Saints in Tarrant Keyneston is a flint church and is Victorian, excepting the Perpendicular, embattled tower. In Domesday the village is Tarent Kaineston. Ralf de Caineto, who came over with William The Conqueror, gave his name to the village. 'Keynes' is derived from 'Caineto'.

The Walk

Go along the road marked to Badbury Rings but do not take this right turn. Instead keep on the hedge-lined lane to Shapwick and its welcoming pub.

*At Shapwick crossroads keep straight on, with the stone cross on your left and the pub on your right. In 350 metres just past handsome Bishops Court Farm, find a path on the left. This leads to meadows and heads west for nearly one mile. At a tarmac road Crawford Bridge is on your left; you turn right along the road for 200 metres then turn left onto a path over a field towards a concrete track. Cross this track and go up to the tarmac road.

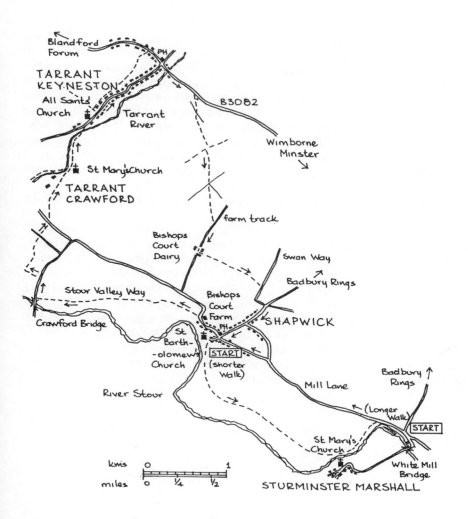

Cross diagonally left and follow the path down into the quiet valley of Tarrant Crawford with its brooding church.

From Tarrant Crawford church continue on the path north and resist the temptation to cross the bridge over the Tarrant. Our path takes us beside the Tarrant River a gushing winter stream which sometimes dries up in the summer, and onto the road at Tarrant Keyneston. Turn right for the village and the church.

After visiting Tarrant Keyneston church, carry on through the village up to crossroads. Turn right and walk on the grass verge beside the B3082 for 250 metres, passing a farm track and a couple of houses on the right. Turn right at a path up through bushes and across a field heading south. In 100 metres there is a kink in the path where it crosses to the other side of the hedge on the right and continues south. Cross a bridleway and in half a mile you reach a farm track. Turn right and walk down this concrete track to some farm buildings. Turn left and head south-east following the hedge on your right. When this hedge deserts you, cross through the middle of the next field to a National Trust stile in the hedge opposite. This takes you into Swan Lane. Turn right on this straight track down to cottages on the edge of Shapwick. Turn left here then immediately right on the Roman road down to Shapwick crossroads.

*At Shapwick crossroads keep straight on to visit the church which overlooks the River Stour.

For the return walk, note that no dogs are allowed here, so people with dogs will have to return along the road which brought them to Shapwick. Otherwise, follow the River Stour back to White Mill on a path not shown on O.S. maps. The Stour Valley Way, here in the hands of the National Trust, has stiles and waymarkng. From Shapwick church cross the car park and head for the river. Bear left over rough ground to a new footbridge. Stour Valley Way leaves the river after the first 400 metres and crosses water meadows. It soon returns to the river where the square tower of Sturminster Marshall church beckons from the other side. We have to stay on the north bank until we reach White Mill and can follow the road over the bridge to Sturminster Marshall.

Walk 38

Tarrant Hinton – Tarrant Gunville – (Farnham – Chettle)

From the quiet villages near the tiny River Tarrant, you go up to Farnham where all the cottages are thatched then on to the hamlet of Chettle, shaded by magnificent trees. This walk can be shortened by omitting Farnham and Chettle. If you do the whole walk you have an opportunity to visit Chettle House, a rare baroque mansion. It is open from April to October, together with gardens and nursery. Phone 01258 830209.

Starting point: The Village Hall, Tarrant Hinton GR937111

Maps: Explorer 118 and Landranger 184,195

Distances: 11 miles or 7 miles if shortened

Terrain: undulating

The Churches

St Mary's is a Perpendicular church on rising ground in a quiet corner of Tarrant Hinton. It has alternating bands of flint and green sandstone. Traces of its Norman origin can be seen in the zig zag over the south doorway. The font is 12th-century Purbeck marble. The battlemented tower, south porch and south aisle make for unity. The church has been well cared for over the centuries and used to belong to Shaftesbury Abbey. In the 14th and 15th centuries, sheep farming contributed to its prosperity. There is a fine sepulcre in Caen stone. The Tarrant Hinton Milennium Committee has commissioned Thomas Denny to design a new stained glass window. You will find it on the left as you enter. The subject of the design is based on Joel Chap.2. In the words of Thomas Denny, 'This passage is full of consolation, promise and renewal, expressed through images of landscape and nature...' The artist has used 'light and vibrant colour' as a 'heightened reflection of the cream/grey green of the stone and flint banded interior'.

St Mary's stands amid trees near the manor house of Tarrant Gunville. The walls of the church, often two feet thick, are of knapped flint and Tisbury stone with some Bath stone. The church was decaying and had to be rebuilt in 1844. Some of the stone may have come from demolished parts of Eastbury House across the road. The porch has the original stone and here there is no flint. The 14th-century archway is still in the porch. The north aisle arcade, of rough Purbeck stone, dates from 1100. The tower is Perpendicular. In the south aisle is a memorial to Thomas Wedgwood, pioneer in photography and son of the great Staffordshire potter. Another son, Josiah owned the manor house here 1799-1805.

Tarrant Gunville church and manor have an elevated place among trees at the
top of the Tarrant Valley

On a hill slope in this pretty Cranborne Chase village of Farnham, the
church of St Laurence has bands of flint and greensand stone. Only the
nave remains of the original Norman church. The tower and entrance
porch are Perpendicular. The rest is Victorian. Nearby is a thatched
lychgate over a well. The Pitt-Rivers museum, now closed was down the
road. It contained local Romano-British and other exhibits. These are now
in Salisbury and Oxford.

   The Church of St Mary is between Chettle House and the little village of
Chettle in the valley. Trees surround them all. The church has bands of
flint and stone throughout. The tower is Perpendicular. The rest was rebuilt in 1850 using the old stone and keeping to the original character. The
fine Baroque house was designed by Thomas Archer and built 1710 by the
Bastard brothers of Blandford. It is red brick with a parapet of Chilmark
stone.

The Walk

From the Village Hall, Tarrant Hinton church can be seen among white,
thatched cottages. They share an elevated corner. Take the lane that curves
past the church and cottages, leading to a footpath. (The right of way goes
north across a field above Tarrant Road). The preferred route apparently is

the wide verge on the right, around the edge of the field. In any case you have to descend to the right-hand corner of the field and then follow a hedge for nearly half a mile.

Turn left onto a stony farm track for half a mile, passing through some farm buildings and then a barn on the right. Continue to the edge of woodland ahead and turn right. Keep to the edge of the wood, heading north again. Join a firm track which emerges from the wood and follow it still northwards. It passes some houses and leads to a Y-junction with finger posts. The path you have just taken is signposted back to Collingwood Corner. Bear right onto Jubilee Trail along a quiet country lane through woodland. Ignore the road to the left at the grass triangle. Keep straight on through a rich canopy of beech, ash and sycamore. The entrance to Gunville Manor is on the right and just beyond, also on the right, is an iron kissing gate leading to the churchyard where St Mary's Church stands peacefully close to the manor.

From Tarrant Gunville church take the steps and path down to the village road. *(It is possible to walk back to Tarrant Hinton from here along the road, distance about one mile)*. More tempting is School Lane opposite. This climbs gently uphill past the school on the left and houses on the right. Look out for the footpath next to a house. It has arrows and 'Jubilee Trail' marked to reassure us. Follow the path through parkland above Eastbury House on the right. Go through a wide avenue and veer left. Climb into a grassy lane and continue north-east. Cross a farm track and follow the field boundary to woodland. Turn left and in a few metres look out for a stile through the hedge on the right. A fine view of rural Dorset opens ahead.

The Longer Route

After crossing the stile *at the viewpoint*, turn left and follow the track to the edge of the field. Turn right and follow the hedge down to a track at the bottom. Turn left and walk along this flat track for less than half a mile, ignoring the path on the right on the way. You come out at New Barn, no longer 'new'. Bear right here and walk along a wide track to Dunspit Lane, which you join at a bend. Bear left.

You can shorten the walk by turning right here and walking along the road to Chettle.

On to Farnham! Continue along Dunspit Lane for half a mile to crossroads. Cross with care and keep straight on into Farnham. The Church of St Laurence is down a lane on the left. You may wish to wander and admire the many thatched cottages in the village.

From Farnham church go down the lane to Museum Hotel. Turn right here and walk along the village street to a road junction. Turn right again and walk gently uphill on the road, also a cycle route. Ignore paths to right

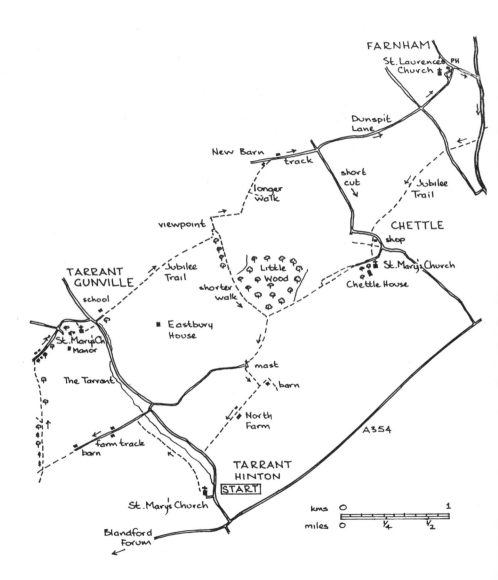

and left. In almost half a mile Jubilee Trail leads off to the right. Turn right here and follow Jubilee Trail south-west across fields with hedgerow on the left. Cross one road and continue on route. In half a mile you can see the trees around the village of Chettle ahead and below. The path becomes a lane down to Chettle. Turn left.

Those who took the short cut also join here.

Pass Chettle village shop and turn right for the church. From Chettle church use the lane alongside going south-west. This passes the public entrance to Chettle House on the left. The lane opens out into a wide grassy space. *Our map shows 2 paths here in anticipation of a planned diversion. It will be well signposted.*

Follow the markers through magnificent scattered trees for half a mile to a Y-junction of paths. Here you leave Jubilee Trail and keep straight on, joining the shorter route described below.

The Shorter Route

After crossing the stile *at the viewpoint,* you turn right and follow Jubilee Trail south with a strip of woodland to the right. In half a mile enter Little Wood on a path which may be muddy in places. At an opening in the wood continue to a junction of paths. Here you leave Jubilee Trail and join the longer route by turning right.

Both Routes

Head south on a well-defined path which leads to a copse. Pass this and turn left at a telecommunications mast. A barn can be seen to the left. In 100 metres turn right and go down a farm lane passing North Farm. In half a mile turn left at the Tarrant road. You are on the edge of the village of Tarrant Hinton. Continue along the road to the starting point at the village hall.

Walk 39

Tarrant Rushton – Tarrant Rawston – Tarrant Monkton

This is a stroll which takes in the pub next door to Tarrant Monkton church. Keep some energy for the return stroll over lovely downland.

Starting point: Tarrant Rushton church GR937060

Maps: Explorer 118 and Landranger 195

Distances: Shorter route returning along the valley road, 6 miles. Longer route returning over downs and visiting Second World War airfield, 10 miles

Terrain: Gently undulating

The Churches

St Mary's, Tarrant Rushton. This is a perfect place; a secluded Norman church on the edge of a quiet hamlet with a rivulet below and downland above. The flint church has been cared for lovingly both now and in the past. There was once a leper hospital of St Leonard nearby and the lepers could watch the church service through the squint. There are three further squints or holes in the wall between aisle and chancel. The chancel also

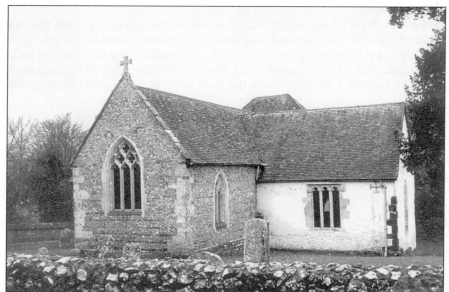

St Mary's, Tarrant Rushton, is a delightful church with many Norman features

has two large earthenware pots built into the wall. These serve to improve the acoustics. The Norman tower stands cosily in the Norman nave.

There once was a church of St Mary at Tarrant Rawston. The tiny building of flint and stone has been absorbed into a private house and can hardly be seen from the footpath.

All Saints, Tarrant Monkton. This flint and stone church has a tower dating from 1200 and windows from 14th and 15th centuries. The rest is Victorian. The church and pub are central to the colourful village of thatched houses. Pack horses stopped here on their way from London to Weymouth. Their three-arched bridge is still here next to the ford.

The Walk

From Tarrant Rushton church go back along the lane and turn sharp right down a footpath past a mill. This narrow footpath takes you to a footbridge over the Tarrant. You then veer right behind the mill garden and cross the field to a bungalow. Scale the stiles and cross the road. Go through the farm gate, bear right and follow the path behind the houses ahead. The path runs parallel to the valley road. Go through the farm buildings at Tarrant Rawston. The little 15th-century church is now sadly redundant and private.

Follow the concrete drive north-east, then tackle the stiff farm gates. Follow the hedge on the left. On reaching the large field, bear right to Luton Farm. Cross the farm lane and continue straight on through the next field to a double stile in the far right corner. Cross the stiles and head due north over three fields to a farm gate. Turn right here and walk down the lane passing large grey corrugated farm buildings on the left. Turn left onto a footpath and bear right, north towards the village of Tarrant Monkton seen ahead. Keep the hedge on your right for 300 metres. Look for a stile in the hedge, cross and there is the church on the opposite side of the field. A pub and restaurant are nearby.

If you wish to visit another Tarrant village continue for half a mile northwards along the valley road to Tarrant Launceston where you may find the site of an old chapel at Higher Dairy.

Both Routes

To return to Tarrant Rushton from Tarrant Monkton church, walk towards the thatched cottages. Just before you reach these cottages, turn right and walk along the village street. In less than half a mile the street bends to the left then to the right. Just past Apple Tree Cottage on the left you come to the Tarrant Road. You have two options.

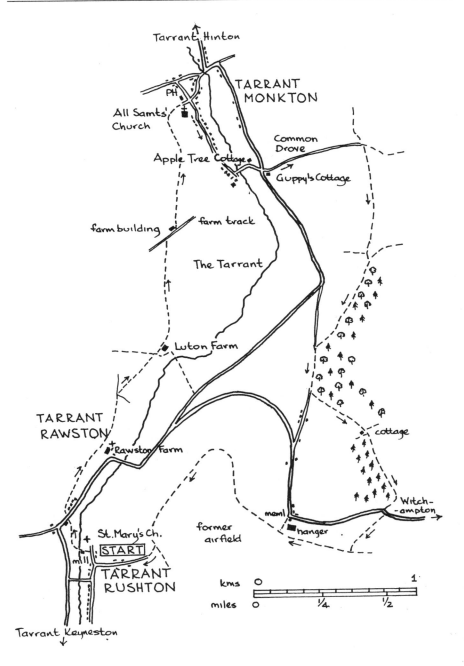

Tarrant Hinton

TARRANT
MONKTON

PH

All Saints
Church

Apple Tree Cottage

Common
Drove

Guppy's Cottage

farm building   farm track

The Tarrant

Luton Farm

TARRANT
RAWSTON

Rawston Farm

cottage

Witch-
ampton

TARRANT
RAWSTON

former
airfield

mewl

hanger

St. Mary's Ch.

START

mill

TARRANT
RUSHTON

Tarrant Keyneston

kms   0   1
miles 0   ¼   ½

Shorter Route

You can walk directly back to Tarrant Rushton following the valley road. There are wide views over the river to the right and Dorset downland to the left. You may see harebells and hawkweed in summer months.

Longer Route

Or you may choose the longer route over the hills. After Apple Tree Cottage cross the road to a track next to Guppy's Cottage. This track, known as Common Drove, goes uphill for 350 metres. At the top turn right but rest awhile to take in the stunning views across Tarrant Valley and the downland beyond. Then head south along a bridleway to a wood and ignore the path to the left. Our bridleway veers right hugging the wood on the left. In about 300 metres, at a T-junction of paths, veer left still keeping the wood on your left. The track becomes firmer and houses can be seen ahead.

Turn left and keep following the edge of the wood. Pass a thatched cottage on the right and ignore paths to left and right. Continue past a dark coppice on your right. The track curves round this and emerges at a tarmac road. Turn left and cross to the bridleway opposite. Keep the fence on your right and in 250 metres turn right onto a very wide track heading north-west. You are now on the site of Tarrant Rushton Airfield. The land has returned to agricultural use but some of the taxiways remain as farm tracks and hangers are used as farm buildings.

Continue north-west past a hanger and ignore the path on the right. Follow the concrete track for a long mile over this plateau. The track swings north, passing an enclosed sump on the left, then south offering views of the ancient hill fort of Badbury Rings. Next, the track veers left and south-east towards a line of evergreen trees, you turn right here. Go through a gate and down a track to the tarmac road which leads to Tarrant Rushton. The church is to the right.

Walk 40

Knowlton Circles – Wimborne St Giles – Gussage St Andrew – Gussage St Michael – Gussage All Saints

This walk delves into Dorset's distant past. The Norman church of Knowlton stands amid prehistoric henges. The path over Harley Down crosses the Roman Road, Ackling Dyke. On Gussage Hill a Celtic farm is close to the longest neolithic cursus in England. 'Gussage' is from Anglo-Saxon 'Gwysych'; gwy = water, sych = dry. This stream dries up in the summer.

Starting point: the verge beside Knowlton Circles off B3078 south of Cranborne. GR023103

Maps: Explorer 118 and Landranger 195

Distance: 12 miles

Terrain: rolling hills and long valleys

The Churches

The lone shell of the Norman church in Knowlton stands in the middle of two prehistoric circular enclosures. Early Christians took over this pagan monument. The church is mainly flint. The 14th-century tower has bands of flint and stone. The church has been deserted ever since the 14th century when it is believed villagers died in the Plague.

In Wimborne, St Giles is a Georgian church, built in 1732 of greensand and flint, some in chequer pattern. After a fire in 1908, Ninian Comper, the architect redesigned the church and endowed it with great beauty. On entry, the font with magnificent cover, designed by Comper makes the first delightful impact. Then the rood screen and loft, with carved figures of the Apostles draw admiration. This is continued in the heavenly roof with a host of angels opening their wings. Next to the church, the almshouses were built in 1624 by Sir Anthony Ashley, later the Earl of Shaftesbury. His mansion nearby is up for sale at the time of writing.

Gussage St Andrew is perfect: simple and retiring. It is a flint building, which replaced the wooden church built from 880 to 893 by St Elfrida, daughter of King Alfred and abbess of Shaftesbury. There was then a nunnery on the site of the farm. The present church has 12th-century herringbone masonry below the west window, near the ground. The window itself is 16th century. Other windows and the door are 13th century. Wall paintings were discovered here in 1951. Most interesting are the 13th-century

Knowlton church – a Norman ruin is surrounded by prehistoric circles

paintings of the Betrayal of Christ, The Crucifixion and the Suicide of Judas.

Gussage St Michael and All Angels has walls of flint and marble with ashlar dressings and some ashlar stone. The lower part of the tower is Norman. Inside the church, the restored Norman tower arch has plain glass doors of 1996. The arcades are Early English, the aisle Perpendicular and the chancel Victorian. Crosses carved on the uprights of the north door are believed to have been made by Crusaders.

Gussage All Saints is 14th century, Decorated style. The chancel was rebuilt in 1860. The lofty tower has been built in three stages: the top is a 15th-century addition in stone, the middle stage has bands of flint and stone, the lower stage is flint. There is an ornate 14th-century Easter sepulcre. The 14th-century font is of Purbeck marble.

The Walk

Go down Lumber Lane away from the main road and heading north-west. The lane goes gently down to the River Allen at Brockington Bridge. The water is so clear that a thriving fish farm with trout is to be seen on the right. Hardy Way, a long distance footpath, crosses the road here. Ignore the path on the left and continue along the road as it curves to the right past the farm. Hardy Way turns to the right here and we follow it north-east along a firm

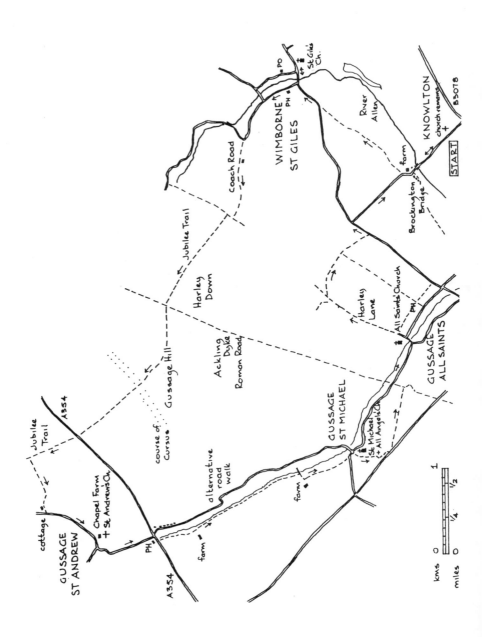

track for 300 metres to a copse. The track becomes rougher, continue along it for a further half mile to a tarmac lane. Turn right here and walk down into Wimborne St Giles. For the moment resist the pub which can be seen down the road on the left. Keep straight on, cross the River Allen again and pass another road on the left which leads to the post office. The church is across the green on the right.

After visiting Wimborne St Giles church, go back to the road with the pub. Go to the end of this road and find the wide bridleway heading north-west. This is Coach Road and passes a monstrous farm building on the left. In half a mile at a T-junction, turn right then left onto Jubilee Trail. This goes north-west with a good hedge on the right. It crosses Ackling Dyke, goes over Gussage Hill with its round and long barrows and crosses the Cursus which cannot unfortunately be traced here on the ground. Ignore all paths to left and right until you have come down and crossed the A354. Opposite is a tarmac lane and Jubilee Trail goes along it. In half a mile leave the trail by turning left onto a path into a field. Follow the hedge on the right but at the second field the path goes between hedgerows. It leads past a cottage to a tarmac road. Turn left and walk along the road for nearly one mile to Chapel Farm. Gussage St Andrew is behind the farm and can be reached by taking the track on the left and climbing some steps.

From Gussage St Andrew continue on the road as it curves south towards a pub on A354. Opposite there is a footpath which runs parallel to the road to Gussage St Michael one and a half miles away. It roughly follows the south bank of the river and there are stiles and waymarks. My experience has been that it is easier to stick to the lane down to the Gussages.

On arrival in Gussage St Michael find the T-junction of roads in the village, the church is nearby. To continue the walk, you can keep heading south-east along the valley road or take the path behind the church. This climbs south-east through the field. When trees come into view, head to the right of the highest tree. Find a stile in the corner of the hedge and continue along the narrow and often overgrown track to the road. Do not cross into the road but follow the fence to a farm gate and stile. Head east for 100 metres and you can then see the tower of Gussage All Saints Church. This should guide you to the Nature Reserve ahead and Ackling Dyke. Turn left and walk along the dyke to the valley road. Turn right at the road into Gussage All Saints. The church is on the left.

On leaving Gussage All Saints take the leafy Harley Lane on the left. This climbs gently and offers lovely views over farm and downland then descends towards woodland. One path branches left. We go straight on for 30 metres then turn right following the track south-east. In half a mile you come down to a tarmac road. Turn left and in 100 metres at a signpost to Knowlton Circles turn right and the church can be seen one mile ahead.

Bibliography

Dorset John Hyams (1970) B.T. Batsford Ltd., London

Dorset Arthur Mee (1939, 1959) Hodder and Stoughton

The Buildings of England: Dorset John Newman and Nicolaus Pevsner (1972, 1997) Penguin

Ordnance Survey, Dorset Compiled by Andrew Bingham, Jarrold Colour Publications

Landranger Guidebook Series edited Peter Titchmarsh (1987) Norwich, NR3 1TR

Discover Dorset Dovecote Press Ltd

Stone Quarrying Jo Thomas (1998) Wimborne, Dorset, BH21 4JD

The Pattern of English Building Alec Clifton-Taylor, Faber and Faber